Unbroken Bond

Tommy Porter

Grosvenor House
Publishing Limited

All rights reserved
Copyright © Ross Porter, 2013

The right of Ross Porter to be identified as the author of this
work has been asserted by him in accordance with Section 78
of the Copyright, Designs and Patents Act 1988

The book cover picture is copyright to Inmagine Corp LLC

This book is published by
Grosvenor House Publishing Ltd
28-30 High Street, Guildford, Surrey, GU1 3EL.
www.grosvenorhousepublishing.co.uk

This book is sold subject to the conditions that it shall not, by way of
trade or otherwise, be lent, resold, hired out or otherwise circulated
without the author's or publisher's prior consent in any form of binding or
cover other than that in which it is published and
without a similar condition including this condition being imposed
on the subsequent purchaser.

A CIP record for this book
is available from the British Library

ISBN 978-1-78148-813-3

This book is dedicated to the memories of my mother, father and my dear brothers and sisters, who will always be with me. I would also like to thank my dear wife, Maureen, for being my rock over the years and for giving me a lovely family. Finally, I'd like to thank my nephew, Ross Porter, who persuaded me to tell my tale and for putting the book together on my behalf. I hope you enjoy my story.

Tommy Porter

Contents

1.	The Early Days	1
2.	The Streets of Bootle	18
3.	The Accident	33
4.	Fun And Games	43
5.	Turmoil	51
6.	Home Again	55
7.	Day To Day	64
8.	The Terrible Twins	71
9.	Bamber Bridge	81
10.	On The Move	93
11.	St. Peter's Catholic School	100
12.	The Great Escape	121
13.	Essex, Here We Come	131
14.	Altar Boy	150
15.	Christmas Cheer	156
16.	At The Seaside	164
17.	On The Move Again	177
18.	Where Next?	194
19.	Summer Camp	216
20.	A Run-In With the Bully	228
21.	Wine And The Spider	238
22.	Wales…Where The Hell Is That?	246
23.	Barmouth	265

Foreword By Ross Porter

This is the story of the childhood of my Uncle Tommy. My late and dearly missed father, Patrick Porter, spoke very little of his childhood and now, having written this book on behalf of his brother, I have more of an understanding why. I am eternally grateful to my Uncle Tommy for sharing the story of his early years.

Unbroken Bond is a compelling story of sadness, love, humour, and of a special bond between brothers that could not be broken. It's a story that simply must be read. Rest in peace, Dad.

Chapter One

The Early Days

My name is Thomas John Porter, and I was born in Bootle, Liverpool in 1940 – a time somewhat different to today.

Our family home at 1a Holywell Road was a three-storey red brick terraced house that was situated on the corner of Irlam Street with part of it extending over a transport cafe. The rooms of our house were large, with traditional high ceilings that were common in this style of property. As was typical in those days, there was no wall paper on the walls in our house but they were painted with whitewash and in some rooms, dots had been added to the whitewash with a sponge to make the walls look more pleasing to the eye. The interior designers of today would have been impressed, I am sure.

I was one of twelve children in a family that consisted of seven boys and five girls. The girls were Edith (Edie – who was the eldest of the girls), Mary, Agnes (Aggie), Joan and Kathleen, and the boys were Michael (Mickey – who was the eldest of the boys), John (Johnny), Steven (Stevie), Patrick (Paddy), Alexander (Alec),

Richard (Richie) and myself, Tommy. There was, on average, about eighteen months between the ages of each of us children. The cobbled streets and jiggers (alleyways) of Bootle were our playground, and I have many fond memories of playing there with my brothers, sisters and friends at the time.

Looking back, I suppose it is fair to say that growing up in the docks area in relatively poor conditions was tough, but it was everyday life for my family and for so many other families who also lived there at the time. We did not complain, and even if we had, there was nobody to complain to and it would not have changed anything. People like ourselves did not know any different, I suppose – that was life back then. As children, we tried to have as much fun as often as possible.

Although some may argue that we had nothing, it may also be argued that we had everything in those days. These were the times when people helped each other: community spirit seemed not only to to exist, but to thrive, and people simply got on with things. Things were either black or white, the world had not gone over the top with political correctness and differences of opinion were often settled by Queensberry Rules and then a handshake. Times were tough, but I guess so were the people.

At the time of my early childhood, in the 1940s, the Porters were a large, well-known and well respected family in the docks area of Liverpool. Many of the family had gone to sea when they were young, and the majority had some connection with the docks and the spin-off industries that revolved around them.

As children, we would sit and watch the dockers walking home from their long shifts in the warehouses that were bursting with cargo from all around the globe. Occasionally, we would also see dockers standing toe to toe and fighting up and down the Dock Road, settling arguments.

Horses and carts graced the streets and competed with the lorries for road space as they carried their goods to and from the depots, railways and canals. Television had been invented, and although we never owned one, I remember being truly amazed when I saw one for the first time. There was a house on our street that had a television and, as kids, we would watch the images on the small screen from outside through their window until we would get caught and chased away. Owning a radio, or wireless as they were known back then, was considered a luxury. Dad had a wireless and we all used to listen intently to the crackling productions and news. I was fascinated by the voices mysteriously coming out of the wooden box and we would spend hours listening to it. Oh, how times have changed.

Like most children, one of my earliest recollections was of my mother – a gentle and kind person who really loved her children. Her name was Edith Porter, and I vividly remember seeing her sitting on the step at the front of the house with her beautiful long dark hair that flowed down to her waist. She was a very pretty lady, and her hair was long enough for her to actually sit on. I can picture her as if it were yesterday, sitting on the front step of our house talking with the other women who lived in Holywell Road.

Edith was born in Bauland Street in Bootle and she had three sisters and two brothers. My father, Richard Porter, was born on Derby Road in Bootle, and he had five brothers and four sisters. As you've probably guessed, large families were the norm in those days – well, they seemed to be in Bootle, anyway!

Holywell Road was always alive with the sound of women talking on their front steps, probably putting the world to rights, and the noise of children playing happily and babies crying seemed to echo around the streets and alleyways. Looking back, there seemed to be babies everywhere, and we would spend hours playing in the street with our mother watching over us from the front step of our house. There were no electronic games in those days, and even if there were, we wouldn't have been able to afford them anyway, so we made our own entertainment and we played outside as often as we could.

As young children, we were not allowed to go too far from the house, as the nearby roads were very busy. Our street joined both Irlam Road and Marsh Lane, which in turn led directly to the docks area of Liverpool – a true industrial area that was also the hub of the city. The docks were a hive of activity and a huge part of our life.

Liverpool had long been considered to be Great Britain's number one port, and its docks were alive with constant activity as the ships rolled in and out carrying cargo to and from countries all around the globe. Liverpool's first dock was built long before my time, in 1715, and it was the first enclosed commercial dock in the world. Once further docks were added, they became interconnected by lock gates extending 7.5 miles along the bank of the River Mersey. Liverpool became the most advanced port system in the world. The clever design allowed ships to move within the dock system 24 hours a day without being affected by the high tides of the Mersey. The people of Liverpool were as proud of their city then as they are today, and rightly so. It is a unique and special place. Although I have not lived in Liverpool for over 50 years, I will always have a special place in my heart for the city.

My family's home was in the tough area of Bootle, and the landscape of Marsh Lane and Rhyl Street that surrounded us mainly consisted of sizeable red brick terraced houses, cobbled streets and large warehouse buildings housing the various shipments that were brought to the docks from all over the world. The traditional terraced houses featured a labyrinth of alleyways. These alleyways provided us children with hours of fun and entertainment. Rhyl Street, which ran next to Holywell Road, was a favourite playground for us, as it had been very heavily bombed during the Blitz. There were large bomb craters randomly scattered throughout the neighbourhood and the crater nearest our house was nicknamed the Debby. I think it took its name from the word debris, of which there was plenty.

Basically, the Debby, our playground, was an area which had been artificially created for us by the highly effective and terribly destructive German bombers that would regularly fly overhead to deliver their cargo of devastation during the Second World War. As I said earlier, people made the best of everything, and we kids happily played in the craters where buildings had previously stood. It is no secret that Liverpool was the most heavily bombed city outside London during the war. Every week, ships arrived in the River Mersey bringing supplies of food and other cargos from the US and Canada and without such supplies, it is believed that Britain would have lost the war. The Germans obviously knew this and Liverpool paid a high price. Hundreds of children across the city played in these newly constructed playgrounds courtesy of our German airborne visitors.

My grandmother, Mary Porter (née Kelly), was known by us all as Granny Porter. She was married to our grandfather Henry Porter. Together, they had six boys and five girls who were all born in Bootle, and my father Richard was the youngest of the boys. Granny Porter lived in a large house on Derby Road, and she always seemed to have plenty of money. Rumour has it that she was a money lender and that she was a formidable character who was not frightened by anyone, man or woman. They say that she even had her own designated table in the local pub, which was unheard of at the time for a woman. My dad spent many times with his mother at the house in which he grew up in nearby Derby Road.

All the other grandchildren of Granny Porter, our cousins, always seemed to be very well dressed and much better off financially than we were. They would always be popping in to see Granny Porter, and she would always make them welcome. When we used to call around to see her, she would always send us straight back to Marsh Lane! It was quite obvious that we were not wanted there, and that she had very little time for the Porter kids from Holywell Road. If we were very lucky when we visited Granny Porter, then we may have had a jam butty (sandwich) before being told to go home. I never worked out why she was like this with us, but her attitude towards us was consistent, to say the least.

The hard-faced Granny Porter was just so different to my other grandmother, Mary Ann Nolan (née O'Brian). Granny Nolan, who was Irish, was a lovely, kind and generous woman who would always make us children feel welcome in her house. Here we were sure of getting a sandwich, a cake and a cuddle every time we visited. Granny Nolan would sometimes even give us three pence to buy some sweets on the way home. I can still see her now in my mind's eye, standing on the doorstep of her house on Borland Street and saying, "Straight home now, boys, as your mother will be wondering where you are." Our grandfather John would then wait on the step until we had left Borley Street safely to enter Marsh Lane on our way home. They were kind and lovely people.

Hours and hours of fun as children were spent playing on Rhyl Street. One of our favourite games as kids was Cowboys and Indians. The bomb craters and building remains had created a landscape which, with a little imagination, was transformed into the prairies of the Wild West of America. Yee-ha!

Myself and my brothers and sisters would play there with our friends from Rhyl Street – members of families such as the McKevitts, the Nugents (who were probably the biggest family in our area at the time), the Rileys, the

Girks, the McDonalds and the Mooneys. There were so many children who used to play there with us and we were lucky to have so many friends, although I cannot remember all of their names now.

My best friend was a lad called John Collins, or 'Yack', as we called him. John lived in Shelly Street and was always in our house with us. Everyone got on well with each other, and the children would play out on the streets until they got called back in to their houses. Our older sisters, Edie or Mary, would be tasked to round us up and get us into the house for food as the evening drew in. We had no clocks or watches in those days, so we would play happily until the bellowing voices of Edie and Mary sounded.

It was Mary's job to give us young ones a good scrub before she helped Edie to cook our tea (evening meal) on most evenings. My sister Mary was also in charge of washing us younger kids and getting us ready for bed. Mary did not really like the idea of having to wash my younger brother Alec and I, as this was never a quick job. We would be as black as soot after a full day playing in the bomb craters. We quickly learnt to approach bath time with caution if Mary was bathing us, especially if she was in a bad mood. Mary adopted a no-nonsense approach to bath time, especially if we gave her some cheek (which was quite often) Thinking about it now, I guess that was the only approach to have taken with such lively children. If we gave Mary any cheek whilst she was bathing us, she would get a bar of Aunt Sally's carbolic soap and rub it in our faces. It tasted awful. If we cried or gave her any more cheek, then she would do it again.

Bath time was not so bad for our elder brother Paddy. He was two years older than me, and he could wash himself. There were no power showers or luxury baths in those days, and we had one tin bath in the house between us all. Children would all have to take turns to scrub in the same water, I hasten to add. There were no hot water boilers in those days, either, and the water to be used in the bath would have to be warmed in pots and pans over the coal fire in the house. Bath time had to be prepared for literally hours in advance. You can imagine how hard it would have been with so many children in our house. Paddy, Alec and I would bath in the same water, and I remember it being almost cold by the time I got in.

Once clean, we would then be off to bed. I shared a bed with Alec and Paddy, and we had one blanket and an old army coat to keep us warm at night. Our bedroom had whitewashed walls and no carpet. We would have to climb the creaky old wooden staircase that spanned the three floors of the house to reach it. During the evenings, my older sisters Edie, Mary and Aggie would undertake the task of repairing our clothes, which would regularly come back ripped from climbing over people's backyard walls, running up and down the jiggers, being a nuisance and general play in our trusted make-believe land of cowboys and Indians.

One of our favourite pastimes was to have a game of football in the street with an old tin can as a ball. If there were no tin can available, then a jumper would be tied up with a ball of string, and we would use that. Despite never having a real football, my childhood was a happy one (from what I can remember almost 70 years later).

School was fun, and the best thing about going to school was that it was here that we would get to play with a real football. Yes, a real football!

My sister Aggie spent most of her younger days with my brother Paddy and his best mate, Siddy McKevitt. Those three spent many times together when they were young, as did Alec and I. My brother Paddy was a lively, loyal and mischievous character right from an early age. So, too, was his best mate Siddy McKevitt. If there were some fun or mischief to be had, then they would be having it, that's for sure. Paddy and Siddy, or the terrible twins, as we used to call them, would often be found arranging fights for our sister Aggie with the other boys who played in the nearby streets. Marbles and sweets were the commodities that were gambled on Aggie's prize fights and more often than not, the boys would come off worse from their tussle with our dear Agnes. Paddy would be the referee, complete with his referee's whistle, and Siddy was her cornerman.

Paddy and Siddy would ensure nobody else got involved with Aggie's title defences and that they were fair fights. I can picture it now, with Paddy using his whistle to indicate the start and finish of every round. Siddy would be the tactical advisor to Aggie between rounds. To be fair to her, Aggie fought well and held her own every time. I suppose it was all good fun, in their eyes at least. Aggie was a bit of a tomboy, to say the least, and if there were any fighting to be done, then she would stand shoulder to shoulder with Paddy and Siddy and fight anyone that dared cross them. Characters, the lot of them.

My brother Paddy got heavily into his boxing, having joined the St James Boxing Club when he was just seven years old. Paddy developed into a very good boxer – the trainers had said he showed an abundance of natural talent at an early age. His left hook became almost famous within the club and he could punch way above his weight. He was fearless. My brother Alec and I were not allowed to go to the boxing club or box, as we were too young, but we used to go and watch Paddy fight down at the club regularly. We would cheer him on to victory at the top of our voices, and we were very proud of him. There were some good fighters at the club at the time, and it had an excellent reputation.

Our Paddy's best mate, Siddy McKevitt, would also spend hours at the boxing gym; they seemed joined at the hip. Both of them could fight well, and were not scared of anyone. Connie McKevitt, who was Siddy's sister, became very good friends with Aggie, and they would often play hopscotch in the street for hours on end. I can still picture Aggie now; playing hopscotch or swinging around the old gas lamps with her knickers tucked into her skirt whilst singing away without a care in the world. There was also Danny McKevitt, Siddy and Connie's younger brother, who hung around with myself and Alec. Our two families were very close, and the children spent a lot of time together.

Although some of us seemed to be playing out all the time, there seemed to be little playtime for my older sisters Mary and Edie. They were always busy cleaning and doing jobs around the house, and never seemed to have any time to themselves. Mary and Edie could often be seen on their hands and knees scrubbing the front step with their old wooden scrubbing brushes as we were playing out having fun. My older brothers, Mickey, Johnny and Stevie, would also be busy with their own lives, so I never really saw much of them whilst I was growing up.

In those days, a popular game for children was playing ollies (you call them marbles these days). Ollies were great, and we would play for hours pushing the little round glass balls around the gutters in the street. We would go for what seemed to be miles, knocking into each other's ollies, laughing and trading various ollies with our friends. Everyone would be after the ollies with the coloured stripes in them, and if you had one of these with green or red in, they were like gold dust. Gold dust that would have to be defended if necessary, as these were my prized possessions, which I wouldn't let anyone in the street take off me. I would share my prize ollies with my brother Alec and Paddy, though, as they would always share theirs with me.

Whilst ollies were a popular pastime amongst the children of that time, the keeping of pigeons was popular amongst the adults. My father seemed to be one of the few men who didn't keep pigeons, but the sight of a pigeon loft (shed) was common in most of the backyards in those days. Rhyl Street seemed to feature the most pigeon lofts, and I recall the best loft being that belonging to Georgie McKevitt, our friends' father. I remember he had a huge pigeon loft, and when we visited the home of the McKevitts, we would often see him sitting in the loft with his beloved birds perched on his hands.

The birds would be in immaculate condition, and you could just tell that he took great care of them – they were his pride and joy.

These were racing pigeons, and I remember seeing Georgie talking to a group of his mates about how the cats were getting into people's pigeon lofts and killing these prize birds. Anyway, I thought nothing more of it until a week or so later, when I caught a fleeting glimpse of the terrible twins: my brother Paddy and Siddy McKevitt (son of the pigeon-loving Georgie) pushing a cat through the letterbox of a boarded-up house that had been a victim of the blitz.

As the weeks went by, I overheard some of the women on the street complaining to each other that their cats had gone missing. They were blaming the local Chinese takeaway for the apparent disappearance of most of the cats in our neighbourhood. Were the terrible twins responsible for such a disappearance? They remained tight-lipped when questioned, and the derelict, boarded-up house was mysteriously burnt to the ground not long after the mystery of the missing felines became the talking point of the streets.

Most evenings, when we should have been tucked up in bed, Paddy, Alec and myself would sneak out of the bed we shared and we would sit on top of the landing peering through the banisters in silence. Our noses would be aching while we watched and listened to the comings and goings of the evening. Our house was always full of people and my dad, Richard (known as Dick) would regularly be talking to what seemed to be a gang of men in the front room in what seemed to be regular meetings. I remember one evening hearing my name being mentioned by one of the men. My ears immediately pricked up, and I thought someone was going to tell on me for something I may have done whilst playing out earlier in the day. I was relieved to hear that I had not done anything wrong, as one of my Dad's friends said,

"I take it young Tommy is named after Nish, then?"

"Yes, that's right," Dad replied.

The conversation then became muffled, to the point that I couldn't hear any more of it. What were they saying and who was this man called 'Nish'?

I often wondered through my life who this 'Nish' person was. Later on, I discovered that I was named after my uncle Tommy, my dad's brother, who was known as 'Nish' to everyone.

Looking back, it seemed that my dad spent most of his afternoons at his mother's house (our Granny Porter), which was situated on the nearby Derby Road. Dad's family lived on Derby Road and generally we would not see our father until he came home in the evenings, after his shift as a fire warden. Mum didn't seem to go out much, but when she did, she would go to visit her mother, who also lived on Derby Road. I remember walking with Mum down a busy Marsh Lane, with some of the shopkeepers coming out to talk to her as we passed. They would all take time out to come out and have a chat with Mum, and they were always nice to us children. If we were lucky, we would be given a biscuit out of the jar at Scott's baker's shop or an apple from one of the fruit and veg shops on the lane. If we were going to visit Granny Nolan (Mum's mother), on Derby Road with Mum, we would always call in to a shop on the corner at the top of Alderly Street.

This shop was called Nelly Dunn's. It has stuck in my mind for years, and I can picture Nelly Dunn right now: she was a woman who was small in stature, with a big heart, and she was always very kind to us. Nelly would lean over her long and large brown shop counter to give us kids a small sweet each every time we went in. Nelly Dunn's shop sold items such as sweets, newspapers, pop and groceries. Her shop was situated on Marsh Lane opposite a pub called The Toolands, which was fondly known as the Stadium by us locals, as there would always be fighting there on a Saturday night. Nelly never had any problems with any of the drinkers from the pub, though, as she was well respected and liked by all on Marsh Lane.

It was obvious that Nelly had watched my mother grow up on Derby Road, and that she was fond of her. When we got to Granny Nolan's house, we would play happily in the street whilst our mother spent some time with Granny Nolan in her house. Our mother never stayed long here or anywhere, really, other than our house at Holywell Street. Mum always seemed to be in a rush to get home to feed us.

I will never forget Nelly Dunn, and I will talk more about her later, because when I returned to Bootle after many years away, sure enough Nelly Dunn's shop was still there and Nelly was again kind to me. I had forgotten a lot about my mum a little later on in my life, but you will understand why when you find out what happened to me and my family.

Because of the events that unfolded in our lives, of which you will learn soon enough, piecing together little snippets of information about my parents has taken some time to achieve. On my parents' wedding certificate, it states that my dad worked on the docks as a labourer and that Mum was a ship's cleaner. I know that in 1940, Dad was a member of the Air Raid Precautions (ARP), and I have a photo from a newspaper cutting at the time with him standing there in uniform with the rest of his unit, which was situated on Derby Road. The report in the newspaper states that the officer in charge of the team had been awarded the OBE after his unit rescued a family that was trapped in a house on Derby Road. An unexploded bomb sat in the surrounding rubble of what was left of the house after it was bombed by the German planes. My dad was a hero in my eyes, whether he was awarded medals for his bravery or not.

Having looked into my family history a little more in the last few years, I have also found out that my dad went to sea as a young man, as many young men from Liverpool did then. Records show that some of them even used the identities and permits of other family members to do so. Some young men, as young as twelve years old, even resorted to jumping ship to different parts of the world as stowaways in search of a better life in a far and distant land. I have documentation to confirm that one of my uncles was caught on board a ship in this way. His excuse was that he was looking for his brother, who had previously left Liverpool as a stowaway and was now living in Australia. My uncle got to Australia and eventually found his brother, who had settled in New South Wales. My uncle then moved to New Zealand after his brother died in Australia. It gives me a warm glow on the inside to know that the Porter family extends itself to both Australia and New Zealand.

Chapter Two

The Streets of Bootle

Growing up in the docks area of Liverpool during the war was tough but fun, and the memories of this part of my life are ingrained in my memory to this very day. One of my earliest memories of the wartime was at bedtime, when my brothers and sisters and I would be standing in complete darkness in the attic of our house, watching from the small window as the docks would be ablaze from the bombings. Searchlights would be scouring the skies above for enemy bombers whilst the sirens wailed into the darkness of the night.

The sound of the bombs going off would make us children jump, and we often hid when the blasts got uncomfortably close. It was like fireworks night almost every night, which I guess was both fascinating and terrifying at the same time. If the raids got too close, then we would all have to evacuate to the trusty nearby air raid shelter across the road from our house. The air raid shelter was a cold concrete structure that was illuminated inside with Tilley lamps. It was generally a scary place to be: kids would be crying with the sound of bombs exploding, and the sirens were wailing whilst we all huddled together to keep safe and warm as it was bloody freezing in there.

In the mornings after such raids, we would rush downstairs or out of the air shelter, depending where we had spent the night, to find our father was still out on duty. I assumed for a while that Dad was a soldier. In fact, he was in the Air Raid Precautions (ARP), which was another name for the wartime fire wardens. I can picture him now standing in the hallway of our house wearing his blue boiler suit and tin helmet. He would be equipped with his trusty gas mask, in preparation of a possible enemy attack from the skies.

The ARP was dedicated to the protection of civilians from the danger of air raids during the Second World War, and its members were responsible for the issuing of gas masks, constructing prefabricated air raid shelters, the upkeep of local shelters and the maintenance of the blackout when the air raid sirens were sounded. The ARP also helped to rescue people after air raids and other attacks and would often have to help to recover bodies – sometimes those of their own colleagues or families. Being in the ARP was a dangerous and important job. That was what our dad did, and we very proud of him for doing so.

The docks were very busy in those days and timber was a popular cargo that was delivered to and stored at the dockland timber yards, of which there were several in our vicinity alone. There was a large timber yard within a stone's throw from our house, and the temptation to sneak underneath the gates to play in this timber yard proved just too much for our little gang from Holywell Road. A striking and very appealing feature of this particular timber yard to us kids was the huge pile of wood shavings that always looked so inviting as it lay on the floor of the yard outside a large workshop. The mountain of wood shavings must have been at least fifteen feet high and ten feet wide and looked almost like a giant pillow. This towering pile of wood shavings was just so inviting to our little gang of friends.

I recall one Sunday, whilst we were playing in the timber yard, curiosity got the better of us, as it so often did. Not content with just playing in the wood shavings, we decided that there was more fun to be had here, so we ventured into the large industrial workshop of the timber yard for the first time to see what we could get up to in there. Entry to the building was gained by way of a rickety old window at the rear, which had been left open by the workers who had rushed to get home earlier. We just had to see where this mountain of wood shavings came from. Was there a big log-munching monster inside that sat there chewing logs all day whilst spewing shavings out into the yard? We just had to find out.

To our amazement, we discovered a huge, nasty-looking machine sitting in the middle of the workshop. This was used to cut the large timber logs into planks. It then churned out the waste wood shavings outside into the yard. The machine was dangerous. It looked dangerous and even smelled dangerous! It had huge saw blades, each of them appearing substantially larger than us. Each blade possessed giant rugged teeth, which looked as if they would cut through anything that crossed their path. There was a nest of belts that drove cogs, which drove the conveyor belts that carried the logs and planks. It was exciting stuff for a kid.

Once we got over the awe of seeing this beast of a machine, Paddy, Alec, myself and our friends were clambering all over it. It wasn't long before we were all walking along the conveyor belts and jumping off the platform at the end of the machine into the wood shavings outside in the yard for amusement. The noise of us laughing and cheering bounced off the old red brick walls and filled the workshop with sounds of glee. How the hell we didn't get killed whilst playing on there I will never know, as there were so many hazards in the workshop, ranging from huge mechanical saws to dagger-like nails scattered on the floor. This venue became a regular haunt of ours until things escalated one day.

Our mate, Matthew Brady, would often volunteer to try things out before we all followed suit. Things like jumping off walls were a normal pastime for our little group of friends. Anyway, on this particular day, he decided to get a plank of wood to slide off the roof of the workshop into the mountain of wood shavings below. He became more keen to prove himself with his intended performance when we fuelled his ego by saying that it could not be done. Now, this was real daredevil stuff, and the anticipation grew as Matthew climbed further up the drainpipe to the roof. Had we done the right thing to encourage him to undertake what was becoming an increasingly dangerous stunt? It was quickly too late to try to talk him down and the small plank was thrown up to him. After taking a couple of deep breaths and some further encouragement from his supporters on the ground, Matthew continued to slide down off the roof, to the sound of cheers.

From the moment Matthew released his grip at the apex of the building, he rapidly gained momentum and he slid down the roof of the building like an Olympic bobsleigh competitor, only without the protection of a bobsleigh or helmet. Within seconds, Matthew was launched skywards, and fell like a sack of spuds off the edge of the roof towards the floor. He seemed to be going so fast, and yet it all seemed to be happening in slow motion; well, at least it was for us watching from the ground. Luckily for Matthew, the stack of wood shavings was underneath the part of the roof from which he had attempted to gain flight. Upon impacting the wood shavings, he quickly disappeared into the heart of the abyss. We could not see our brave friend, but we could hear him screaming and thrashing about inside the pile. A rescue mission was quickly undertaken whilst we tried not to wet ourselves laughing. We lived for moments like this.

Much to Matthew's delight, our rescue mission was successful and we recovered the bedraggled and bruised body of our friend. We brushed him down as best we could and tried to remove the largest of the splinters that stuck out of him like a porcupine before we took him back to our house. Once at our house, we patched Matthew up some more and gave him a drink of water before he headed home after his ordeal. At least he was in one piece and still alive to tell the tale. There was a park that we could have played in on Marsh Lane, but it was very rare that we ventured down there when we were little, as it was too far from the house and we weren't allowed to venture that far. Anyway, at that particular time, who needed a park when we had timber yards to play in?

Another landmark of Holywell Road that I remember vividly was the large air raid shelter that was situated across from our house. We seemed to spend an awful lot of time huddled in this shelter. I recall one winter's evening when I was sitting in our front room with my brothers and sisters whilst our mam was cooking a large pan of scouse (stew) to feed us all, when the noise of the air raid sirens boomed out around the streets. The wailing of the sirens had become so familiar to us – we all knew instantly that this meant an attack from above was imminent. As we so often did, we all dashed out of the house, with our mother desperately trying to round up the younger siblings quickly to make our way to the safety of the trusty air raid shelter. I remember being scared whilst running behind my mother as she dragged my younger brother Alec by the hand across the road.

There was chaos, and there seemed to be people making a mad dash to the shelter from every direction as the German bomber engines grumbled closer from above. As we hastily made our way to the shelter, Mum dropped her purse in the mayhem and several pennies bounced out on to the floor. She carried on to the air shelter and shuffled us kids into the hut before she ran back onto the road to pick up the pennies that had fallen from her purse. All the neighbours and kids screamed from the shelter, "Come on Edie, get in here. The Germans are coming."

Mother ignored their pleas and continued to collect the pennies, in what can only be described as an act committed out of bravery and sheer desperation. With hindsight, I can now see why she did what she did and understand just how precious those pennies were to us as a family. We were poor, and a couple of pennies made a big difference – we could not afford to lose any money whatsoever. Times were hard and brave actions were called for. I am pleased to say that our mother made it to the shelter safely on this occasion. The door of the shelter was slammed shut and we awaited the noise of the overhead bombers and the deployment of their cargo of destruction and death.

What seemed like the residents of the entire street sat in the shelter. It was pitch black inside, and it was cold. Babies cried whilst mothers tried to console them as the engines of the German bombers grumbled like giant angry bees in the sky above us. We could hear the whirring of the bombs dropping from the planes onto our beloved streets and houses and the sound of the bombs exploding echoed through the streets of Liverpool. With each explosion came more fear for us kids, as we could not see what was going on, which led to imaginations running wild and cold sweats were a plenty. All I knew was that the explosions seemed close by and that I was glad to be with my family at such a scary time. Another worry was that our dad was out there during the bombing, and we prayed, as we did every time there was a raid, that he was also safe from harm as we held hands tightly.

After being huddled together for what seemed to be hours and having been given the all clear, we ventured out of the bomb shelter to find that, as it was travelling on its journey of destruction, a German bomb had taken the chimney clean off a house in our street and had continued to totally obliterate three houses in the next street, Rhyl Street. Further on from Rhyl Street was Marsh Lane, on which there was a library and public baths. These were also destroyed by the latest in what seemed like a never-ending series of German bombings of Bootle. Fire engines were present and people swarmed around the blazing sites in an attempt to put out the fires and to rescue anyone who may have been caught out in the raid and of course, to retrieve the bodies of the dead. Memories like these stay with a person forever. Our mother took us back home that night and we went to bed having survived another attack.

Looking back on being a small child during the Blitz, in a strange sort of way, it was amazing to think that we were so close to being killed by the bombs on so many occasions and that I survived to tell the tale. The air raid shelter on Holywell Road was like our second home, and it all was just part of everyday life at the time. If you have lived through those times, then you can't help but feel for those families whose fathers or other relatives did not come home to them. The war was a sad time for so many people, and it surely engraved memories that must never be forgotten. Neither should the bravery of our soldiers and civilians who lost their lives defending our nation.

I am not sure if this was a sign of the times or not, but our dad had a policy when it came to us kids playing out. Dad was a straight-talking man's man who would take no nonsense from anyone, and his playtime policy was based on a simple rule. You were either playing in or out of the house. Dad did not do in between. This policy was strictly adhered to by all of us children, even in the winter. If we decided to go out in the morning to play, then even if it was lashing down with rain, we had made our choice and we were out for the day. If we chose to stay in, then that was fine, but we would not be allowed outside to play for the day. Decisions had to be made carefully. We preferred to play with our mates in the street most of the time, probably as we could get up to more mischief this way.

As I have said, I was one of 12 children and times were hard for our family as they were for many, many other families in Liverpool at the time. I remember being cold outside whilst playing in the street in the winter with my little black galoshes (you would call them deck shoes or pumps today) with the snow up to my ankles and my feet bloody freezing. My backside would be hanging out of my pants as they were constantly being ripped, repaired by my sisters or mother and ripped again during everyday playtime activities. It must have been so difficult for my mother and father to try to raise 12 kids in such conditions of what can only be described as utter poverty. This was the norm for us and we knew no different, so we tried to make the best of every situation and we appreciated everything.

To say there were few luxuries in life was an understatement, but we did have each other and a lot of love from our parents, so I guess we had a lot, really – a lot more than others who may have been financially better off, but never felt as content and loved as we did. I fondly look back and recall sitting in front of an open fire on a winter's night, staring into the flames as they heated a pan of water which was to be used to fill the tin bath for us kids to wash in. The big black fireplace dominated the front room complete with its brass fittings either side of the grate. The fireplace was an impressive feature of the room but it wasn't a popular feature with my elder sisters, Edie, Aggie and Mary. It was their job to keep this large, ornate fireplace clean and they would spend hours and hours polishing the fireplace with what we used to call 'black lead' until you could literally see your face in it. It was a painstaking and tedious task to keep this fireplace in almost showroom condition, but they did a great job.

Our house was basic, but clean. We had no fancy furniture, but we did have a table and chairs to sit around to eat. There was no tablecloth and the table was scrubbed white – again a task which my sisters completed to a high standard, and occasionally if people were visiting the house we would put newspaper on the table to make it look more presentable. The *Liverpool Echo* would double up as our tablecloth for entertaining. The floors were wooden and were meticulously scrubbed clean by Edie, Aggie and Mary. To be fair, those girls worked very hard indeed.

Our house seemed like a meeting place for many local people, as the evenings would often see friends or associates of my dad sat in the front parlour discussing various topics with him. More often than not, the topic of conversation between my dad and his visitors seemed to be politics. Alec and I would hear them talking about the government as we peered sneakily through the banisters, busy listening to their conversations in the evenings when we were supposed to be tucked up in bed. We would hear mumbled voices and occasionally those voices would be raised, as the debates got a little heated at times. Despite this, Dad's visitors would always end the evening with a handshake with him at the front door on their way out. Alec and I wouldn't miss a trick. There seemed to be dozens of men leaving the house sometimes, much to our fascination.

I remember one time when our front parlour was bursting with what seemed to be enough placards to start a revolution from our own house. These placards had been made out of large square pieces of hardboard and long pieces of timber and they featured handwritten posters that said, "Vote For Mr Kinley." My siblings and I would accompany my dad and his associates around the streets of Bootle, Litherland and surrounding areas singing a song that went like this, "Vote, vote vote for Mr Kindley. Who's that knocking on the door? Let him in and kick him in the shin and he won't come voting anymore."

We would sing that at the top of our voices for hours and our little army of tuneful marchers would grow steadily as it snaked around the streets of Bootle. This went on for at least two weeks and our throats would be dry and voices almost horse after our marathon sing-along. Unlike today, there were no expensive election campaigns for local politicians and every night, we would happily join forces with other gangs of kids from neighbouring streets and march up and down Marsh Lane singing the "Mr Kindley" song. I remember it as if it were yesterday.

Mr Kindley was a local Labour councillor and he did get elected, so I like to think that we played a little part in his success – we sung our hearts out and our feet were sore after all the walking we did. Election day came around, and to celebrate Mr Kindley's success and the support of all concerned, there was a big party in our house. There seemed to be dozens of men there drinking, smoking and being merry. My mother wasn't participating in any of the celebrations, as father didn't allow her to smoke or drink. I guess that is just how it was in those days. My dad was obviously involved with local politics, as he was always being called upon and would regularly attend meetings. He was known to speak his mind and would commit himself to any campaign fully.

There was no television in those days, and the home entertainment was provided by listening to the wireless (or radio, as it is known as today). I remember being fascinated as a child hearing the voices and music coming out of the radio and wondering just how they did that. It seemed like magic when I heard them for the first time. The wireless was probably our biggest luxury item, and we all loved it. There were no electric lights in our house but we had gas mantles for internal lighting. Half the time we could not afford to buy the mantles (a mantle was the wick part of the gas lamp that burned to give off the light), so our eyes got used to the dark! For most of the time we relied upon these little Tilley lamps and candles strategically positioned around the house to give us enough light when darkness crept in.

Although our possessions and facilities may have been basic, there were always books and comics around the house, whether they were from the library or school. I always enjoyed reading. All of us children could read before we started school, which was quite impressive in those days. Mum would sit with us all and read with us, which was not an easy task when there was so many in the tribe. I guess nothing was easy for our mother with so many children in the house. I remember spending hours as a child being glued to comics like the *Dandy* and the *Beano* and laughing out loud at the antics of the characters in the publications. Dennis the Menace was a favourite of mine.

The only job that I can remember my dad having was that of a fire warden. He would come home every night around about 9:30 p.m., assuming there were no air raids going on – otherwise we wouldn't see him until the next morning. We could have set our watches by his routine – if we would have had any watches, that is! Myself and my brothers and sisters would all look down the street to wait to see him walking home to our house on Holywell Road. My father was a strong, tall man who would always walk with his hands behind his back and he would walk with a straight back and a confident swagger.

We would always watch intently whilst he walked home. When Dad was carrying something, then our spirits were lifted, as we all knew that there would be food that evening. A top treat was corned beef and potatoes that Dad would have 'obtained' from down the docks. I recall enjoying what seemed to us kids at the time as a big banquet on such occasions. If we were really, really lucky, then we would have a big bowl of chips from, Joe Logan's chippy (fish and chip shop) for our evening meal. That was bliss.

Joe Logan's chip shop was situated halfway down the street. Our Paddy would often go and collect the food from the chip shop and bring it home to satisfy the hungry mouths in the house. We would all sit at the table and then pile into them from one big bowl that would be placed at the centre of the kitchen table. Feeding a family of 12 children in those days was no mean feat (neither was carrying so many bags of chips back home to a starving brood without dropping them on the way). Well done, Paddy. There would have been murder if he had dropped them. Sometimes, us kids would hang about outside waiting for closing time, as Joe was very kind and always gave us Porters a big bag of batter bits to take home. Batter bits butties (sandwiches) were delicious!

Clothing the family was also a challenge for my parents. If we were lucky enough to have a pair of shoes, then it was up to us to look after them. They would simply have to last, as we couldn't have another pair. The shoes would be used for all our activities, which ranged from going to school, climbing walls, running up and down jiggers to playing football and go-cart racing, and would inevitably get torn. Despite this multitude of uses, if we ripped our shoes and even if our toes were sticking out of the front of them, then it was tough luck, as we were still wearing them to school and walking in the sun, rain or snow in them. There was no choice. If we complained to Dad, then he would simply say that it was our own fault for not looking after them in the first place We might even get a clip around the ear for complaining. Later in life, I realised that our parents really struggled to afford to buy items such as shoes and clothes for so many children.

Dad was not a violent man, but he certainly was a strict disciplinarian and would stand for no nonsense from us kids or from anyone, really. I remember going in to the house one day with tears rolling down my cheeks and crying to my dad because one of the other children on the street had hit me. Dad continued to clip me around the ear and he told me to get back out there and hit them back and not to come back in until revenge had been sought. That's just the way it was for us, and all of my brothers and sisters and I grew up fighting in one way or another. The kids in the street soon realized not to pick on me or any of our clan, as we would always have a go back at them and would not back down from anyone. We would also stick together and fight toe to toe with anyone, which put a few people off messing with us, I am sure.

Chapter Three

The Accident

When I reached the age of five, I was entitled to go to St James School – a Roman Catholic Church School situated on Marsh Lane in Bootle. One of the big perks and main attractions of going to school was the fact that we would get fed at dinner time, as well as trying to learn things, of course. St James School was a big school with a catchment area that almost spanned the entirety of Bootle, and there must have been hundreds of children attending. All pupils would have to go to mass every Sunday and on every saint's day, and I remember bringing home tins of milk for the babies, tins of cocoa mixed with sugar, and orange juice from what I remember to be some sort of a welfare unit attached to the church.

I must confess that temptation often got the better of me and I would regularly open the tins of sugar and cocoa on the way home. Alec and I would sneakily taste test the contents as a little treat. Having committed our act of naughtiness, Alec and I would then carefully put the lid back on the tin before arriving home, and we would pretend that the journey home had been uneventful if asked. Unbeknownst to us, our faces would sometimes feature noticeable traces of cocoa, which was a bit of a giveaway. As a result, we had several tellings-off for this. The cocoa was lovely, though, I must admit, and well worth the rows.

My brother Alec and I were always together. He was almost like my shadow: wherever I went, he went with me. We were inseparable. I was seven years old and Alec was five years old, when one day when I was making my way to school. Alec followed me out of the house and down the street. Usually, my mother or eldest sister, Edie, would keep Alec in and stop him trying follow me to school, but on this particular day, Alec decided that he was going to follow me no matter what, and had crept out of the front door without anyone knowing.

As I was walking on to the bustling Marsh Lane, for some reason, I felt the urge to look back and when I did, I saw my little brother Alec and Lady (our dog) walking behind me. I kept shouting,
"Go home Alec, you can't come with me, lad."
I crossed the busy road and he was the other side of the road on the pavement and Alec was shouting back to me,
"I want to come with you, Tommy. Wait for me."
I replied again with, "You can't come with me Alec so you'd better get home now."

If Alec had listened to my advice and was starting his journey home, I turned my back and continued with my walk to school. Before I knew it, I heard an incredible sound of screeching brakes and bloodcurdling screaming.

I immediately felt sick to my stomach and felt my complexion instantly turning as white as a sheet. I knew something terrible had happened and chances were that my dear little brother would not be far away from the incident. My head spun around faster than it had ever done before, to see that that a lorry had hit Alec, who had made the mistake of trying to cross the road. The brakes of the lorry continued to omit a heartbreaking screech, and I could see poor Alec getting dragged along the cobbled street in severe agony. He had somehow had become tangled in one of the rear wheels of the vehicle. Alec was stuck between the rear wheel and the rear wheel arch, and it did not look good for him.

The lorry eventually stopped in what seemed to be an eternity that passed by me in slow motion. Within seconds, people swarmed out of their houses like ants and rushed to the scene of the accident in an attempt to help my brother. I sprinted over to Alec with tears running down my cheeks and with my heart beating like a giant drum inside my little chest, but I could not get near my little brother due to the sheer number of people surrounding what was the scene of a shocking accident. Blood appeared to be everywhere. The road was red and I sobbed relentlessly as I watched men trying to free Alec from this carnage. I have never seen so much blood to this day. The ambulance eventually came and by this time, someone had run down to our house to notify our mother of the accident.

Panic set in and Mother, Edie, Aggie and Paddy appeared at the scene in no time at all. My mother held Alec in her arms until the ambulance came and took him away to

Bootle General Hospital on Derby Road. Everybody was upset and there was an eerie atmosphere of sadness. We all felt so helpless. The hospital where Alec was taken was easily a good mile and a half away from the scene of the accident. This did not stop my mother as she ran whilst pushing her pram all the way to the hospital in a bid to be there for Alec. In those days, the ambulances were not so well equipped and were smaller than the vehicles of today, and having the opportunity to ride in the ambulance with the patient was just not possible. I remember vividly to this day, after the ambulance had taken Alec away to hospital, picking up one of his shoes to find that it was full of blood and the sadness of us all in the aftermath of what was a horrific accident. I can still see that little shoe full of blood when I recall the accident, even today.

I did not see Alec for what seemed an eternity at the time, but it was more like several weeks when I look back now. We all missed him dearly, especially Paddy and I. Alec was hospitalised for months and had been in a bad way as a result of his encounter with the lorry. The accident had left him recovering from a massive loss of blood and a catalogue of serious injuries. He was lucky to survive. Apparently the surgeons who dealt with him when he arrived at the hospital thought he was likely to die and warned my mother to expect the worst. Alec defied all odds and he survived. When Alec eventually came home, he sported a massive scar on the back of his head in the shape of a horseshoe, his ankle had been totally mashed up as a result of having been tangled in the wheel arch whilst being dragged down the road. He had lost two middle fingers on his left hand, and he seemed to be almost wrapped head to foot in bandages like an Egyptian mummy. At least we had our brother home alive, albeit in a somewhat sorry looking state.

We were all very pleased to have Alec home. Initially, upon his return from hospital, Alec was confined to the house, as he obviously could not walk in the state he was in. Our little gang of mates on the street decided that we would make Alec a cart so he could come out to play with us and we could pull him behind us wherever we went. We searched high and low for a set of pram wheels (finding such wheels was like finding the winning lotto ticket today – they were certainly a commodity in demand in those days, amongst us kids, anyway). Our crew obtained two boxes that had been used to store oranges in from the jigger of the local fruit and vegetable shop and Alec's cart was constructed. One box acted as the driver's seat and the other was the rear passenger seat where Alec would sit. Despite his injuries, Alec showed incredible bravery and would come everywhere with us in his customised chariot until he became well enough to resume normal activities.

One thing that has always puzzled me later on in life is what happened to the compensation money that was awarded to Alec as a result of his horrendous accident at such an early age. He was just five years old when he got run over by the lorry and suffered those horrific injuries and as a result of this, he was awarded compensation, which we were led to believe to be around five thousand pounds in total. This was a lot of money in those days and would probably be equivalent to around £45,000 in today's funds. Apparently this compensation was to be put into a trust fund, which Alec would then have access to when he reached the age of 21. As kids, Alec would always say to me, "Don't worry Tommy, when we grow up, I will be rich and we will have many new clothes. I'll look after us – don't worry, mate."

Sadly for Alec, when he reached the age of 21 and went down to Bootle Town Hall accompanied by our eldest brother, Mickey, to collect his compensation, he was informed that the amount remaining in his trust fund was just £500. Alec was obviously gutted when he found this out. Where had his compensation gone? He had looked forward to this day for over a decade, and when he asked where his compensation had gone, the well dressed man behind the desk at the town hall told him that the money had previously been withdrawn to help the children of the family through the difficult times during their childhood. I guess we will never know what happened to the compensation money, but someone other than Alec obviously had it.

At school, and despite him having lost his two middle fingers on his left hand, Alec was really good at gymnastics, as was our Paddy. I was happy to kick a homemade football around and Aggie and Mary enjoyed playing their netball. Mary and Aggie both played for the senior teams of the school and they would often play in competitions against other schools. I remember watching one such match with my father from outside of the school, through the railings on Marsh Lane. Further down from us, a small group of teenage boys had gathered and were cheering and shouting at the girls as they tried to maintain concentration on their all-important match.

Dad was obviously not pleased with the attention both Mary and Aggie were getting from the group of teenagers, and just as he started to walk towards the group to express his dissatisfaction with their cheering and leering, the nun who was refereeing stopped the game and told the boys in no uncertain terms and in her sternest voice to go home, and clearly stated that she would not restart the game until they had done so. The group of boys dispersed and the netball match continued with a victory for the team of St James School.

My sister Aggie was also in the local morris dancing troop. Morris dancing was a popular pastime in those days and her troupe, like many others, used to make all of their own costumes to perform in. In those days, the costumes were made out of colourful crepe paper. The Marsh Lane Morris Dancers would take part in all the local carnivals and competitions. I remember once when Aggie came home crying her eyes out as the heavens had opened and it had lashed down with rain in the middle of their competition. She was furious. All the dye from her crepe-paper costume had run all in her hair, over her face and everywhere, really. She looked like all the colours of the rainbow, but with a face like thunder!

The older we became, the further afield we would venture to play to gain our kicks. One winter's day, our little group of mates decided to go and play up at Bibby's Lane for a change. Bibby's Lane was famous in Bootle. Legend had it that a man could be seen driving his horse-drawn coach and horses whilst holding his head under his arm up the lane if you visited it in darkness. All the kids near us knew of the legend and it is safe to say were all terrified (although they all pretended not to be). Our little group that day, with Alec in his specially built cart, went up to Bibby's Lane as the late afternoon light was fading and we all sat there listening and watching for any strange goings-on.

Sure enough, it was not long before the sound of horses trotting on cobblestones was heard, and we all ran home screaming in fear for our lives. We did not realize it at the time, but the noise of the trotting horses was coming from the nearby dock area. However, we were convinced that the man with his head under his arm was coming for us, so we legged it. A visit to Bibby's Lane, to scare ourselves silly, became a weekly occurrence for quite some time. The tings you do as a kid for amusement!

Another favourite place to visit, before it got too dark and someone would be out looking for us to get us back in to our house, was the cemetery at the end of our street. As many cemeteries are to children when frequented in the fading daylight, this cemetery was a spooky place to be, but we were morbidly fascinated with it. Whilst walking around the graves reading the names and verses in an attempt to scare each other, we found one headstone that looked particularly spooky. This gothic-style headstone had the words, "I am not dead, I only sleep," chiselled into it. One of the older boys in the group would read this out to us in a slow and scary voice and more often than not, a cat or some other sort of creature would rustle in the bushes and we would run home screaming yet again. Great fun.

The summer months always brought mischief and I remember on one Saturday morning about six of us kids walked what seemed to be a marathon to the town of Ford. Someone had tipped us off that there was a large orchard full of apples just waiting to be scrumped (stolen), so those apple trees became our target for the day. After our epic walk to the orchard, sure enough our tip off had been correct and our little group of scrumpers quickly relieved as many trees as it could.

The apple rustlers left the scene with as many apples as we could carry and we had apples stuffed down our jumpers and anywhere else we could fit them in. We were gutted when we got home and found the apples to be the sour-tasting variety that we called crab apples, as opposed to the edible type. Our mission to bring back a consignment of the finest apples was a failure. We had nothing to show for our marathon walk but blisters on our feet, an upset stomach and a tale to tell.

One of my favourite days out as a child was a trip to Seaforth Sands, or the shore, as we used to call it. Seaforth Sands was a popular destination for a summer day out for families in our area. The Porter family would get together with the McKevitts, the Nugents and the Rileys. Each family would have bottles of water and loaves of dried bread, and off we would go for a day playing on the beach. Once at the beach, the boys would make a dash for the old military pillboxes that were positioned along the seafront, where we would happily play soldiers for most of the day.

For those of you who do not know what a pillbox is, it is a concrete dug-in guard post that was normally equipped with small gaps in the wall, through which the soldiers or Home Guard would fire their weapons. The pillboxes because of their similarity to the cylindrical and hexagonal boxes in which medical pills were once sold. About 28,000 pillboxes and other hardened field fortifications were constructed in England in 1940 as part of the British anti-invasion preparations of the Second World War, and it is said that some 6,000 of these fortified structures remain today in the UK. We had great fun at the shore in summertime, and I often find my mind wandering back to those happy days.

Chapter Four

Fun and Games

A visit to our street by the rag and bone man was always eagerly anticipated by us kids. He would walk up and down the streets shouting, "Any old rags, any old rags, any old rags," and he would go into people's houses to collect their old rags or any old junk that they wanted to dispose of. We used to watch him like hawks, and if he had any bike or pram wheels on his cart, then when he went into one of the houses, we would make a dash for his cart and pinch the wheels. We would have to be careful, though, as the rag and bone man would not be best pleased if he caught us. Wheels were a valuable commodity on the streets of Bootle.

Pram wheels would be used to make go-carts, and if we managed to pilfer a bike wheel, then we would get a stick and run up and down Marsh Lane hitting and steering the wheel with it. We soon mastered the art of running with the bike wheel and had regular races around the block to see who was the fastest at this newly formed Olympic sport. Our raids on the rag and bone man's cart provided hours of pleasure.

There was also a competition to see who could build the best go-cart. Once they were built, our test track was at Coffee House Bridge, which was quite steep. Passersby would often see us kids hurtling down the road, and nine times out of ten, we would smash into something at the bottom and overturn. It may be argued that we were pioneers of the crash test dummy. Marsh Lane station was also a favourite haunt with our newly made and highly tuned go-carts, as the station had a steep tunnel running up to it and big gates at the bottom.

Much to the annoyance of the daily commuters and the staff at the station, we would pull our go-carts up to the top of the incline as far as we could, which was by the pay desk by the entrance to the platforms. Once at the top of the incline, we would then come hurtling down the hill in our customised racing carts into Marsh Lane before sticking our feet out to drag along the floor to stop the cart before catastrophe struck.

Every now and then our little gang of friends, which was headed up by Paddy and Siddy, would pay a little visit to The Palace picture house on Marsh Lane. Entrance to The Palace was about sixpence. This was quite a lot of money in those days – well, it was for us, anyway – so we used to all club our money together to allow one person to buy a ticket and to enter the picture house. Once inside, our stooge would then find a seat, and when the usherette had turned their back, he would go straight to the toilets to open the emergency doors at the back of the picture house. We would all then flood in to take our seats ready for the film.

Over time, the usherettes cottoned on to our little scam and if we got bubbled then they would, much to the annoyance of the paying customers, stop the film and continue with a great hunt for us kids. They would shine their flashlights in every nook and cranny, while we would all split up and hide anywhere possible, including under seats and under people's coats and clothes. Some people would obviously feel sorry for us having to bunk in and would try to help us hide by putting their coats over us so the usherettes could not find us. Nine times out of ten, we all got caught and were thrown out without having watched the film. It was great fun, though, I must admit.

When we could afford to go to the picture house and opted for the conventional paying method of entry, it would be on a Saturday afternoon, as that was the cheapest time to go. We loved to watch the cowboy films, which starred people like Tom Micks and Gabby Hays. One of my personal favourites was *The Lone Ranger*. After watching the film, we would run all the way home from the picture house to our street whilst slapping our bottoms, pretending that we were riding horses and shooting imaginary guns at each other in the process. To quote the old saying by many a grumpy old man, "The kids today don't know they're born."

Holywell Road was full of children playing together. The neighbours were kind to each other, and everyone got along well. Our house featured two bedrooms on the first floor. It was situated above a café that was owned by two sisters. There were always horses, carts and lorries parked outside the cafe whilst the workers from the docks had food inside.

There was a cellar with an adjoining door between our house and the café at the top of the stairs. It was a thick old wooden door that was bolted closed from the cafe side.

The interconnecting cellar door had two bolts securing it. I know this because often on a Saturday evening, if we listened carefully, we would hear the two bolts sliding open as the sisters would kindly leave a tray of sandwiches or cakes for us on our side of the door. I assume that these were the leftovers from the café that had not sold, but this did not bother us kids. Looking back, I can see that the sisters who owned the cafe obviously felt sorry for us. They were kind-hearted souls.

Dad would not have been pleased and he would have surely refused the food if he had known what was going on. Dad was far too proud a man to accept such charity. Paddy and I would listen for the noise of the bolts and wait until Dad had gone out before the food parcel was collected and its contents devoured. The empty plate would then be put back by the door. The noise of the bolts opening would again be heard and the plate would be taken back by the sisters. They were very kind to our family and helped us whenever they could.

Our family was poor, but we had some form of a meal every day. We were happy, and we had clothes on our back, albeit clothes that may have been a little worn. I would always get the hand-me-downs from my older siblings. Many families shared these experiences in those days. Times were hard, but that was just the way it was. Living hand to mouth was part of everyday life, but it did not stop us having fun.

Looking back, I now realise that Mum did not seem to sit out on the step anymore by this time. She would be in bed in the front parlour, so we would have to be quiet in the house or if we played directly outside our house to allow her to rest peacefully. If we made a noise, then either Father, Edie, Aggie or Mary would tell us keep quiet. My brother Paddy was a bit older than me and Alec and was always out with his best mate, Siddy McKevitt, and his other mates like Terry Riley, Yack Collins and the Carr boys.

When I cast my mind back to my early childhood, I now realise that the eldest of the girls in our family, Edie and Mary, really had quite a hard time of it as teenagers. As I have said, they were responsible for all sorts of duties around the house, from scrubbing the floors to scrubbing the younger children. Their teenage years were mostly spent working in this way and they had very little time to enjoy themselves, really. Father was strict and neither of them were allowed to wear any make-up – and there was no way that any boys would ever be allowed to come knocking at the door for them, that's for sure. Both of them worked very hard and played a big part in taking care of me, so I have a lot to thank them for.

My brother Paddy seemed to be my father's favourite, and he used this to his advantage at times. As I have said earlier, Paddy was a lively character, who was always up to something or other, but he was a fun big brother to have around. Paddy was always there to look after Alec and I. When we had been naughty, we would be sent up to bed by our mother, but as Alec, Paddy and I shared the same bed, this form of punishment would turn into the three of us bouncing on our beds in fits of laughter. Upon the return of our dad, mother would tell him who had been naughty and what they had done. Dad would then come upstairs and chastise the culprit or culprits. Nine times out of ten, it would be Paddy, because he was that little bit older than Alec and I, and was definitely the ringleader.

The bed that we three brothers shared had seen better days, and the regular bouncing had taken its toll on the mattress structure. The mattress developed a dip in the middle, and Paddy often used this dip to his advantage. We would hear the heavy footsteps coming up the old wooden staircase and we all knew what was coming next: the dreaded belt. Dad would take his leather belt off his trousers and whack us across our bums or backs as we lay in the bed as punishment for our earlier antics.

Unbeknownst to Father, Paddy would have crawled into the safety of the dip in the mattress, thus using Alec and I as human shields. Alec and I would be howling in pain whilst Paddy would be acting as if he was also getting the belt. Once Dad had gone back downstairs, Paddy used to say to us, "Never mind, lads, I'll make it up to you."

Our Paddy was always as good as his word and he would make it up to us. He would always look after Alec and I if we had any problems with anyone, and he would always share any goodies that he would come home with from his little outings or scams with his partner in crime, Siddy McKevitt. Paddy and Siddy would often appear with treats ranging from exotic fruit to ice cream. Paddy, Alec and I were very close and had a strong bond. We felt like the Three Musketeers when we were together as kids, and Paddy would always see to Alec and I first, whatever the situation. This continued throughout our adult lives.

Our sleeping arrangements were always going to be a little cramped, with so many of us living in the same house. Besides Paddy, Alec and I sharing a small box room (and a bed), Edie, Mary and Aggie had their own room and the babies, Joan, Richie and the youngest, Kathleen, would sleep in another room with my mum. I remember seeing my younger brother, Richie, as a baby fast asleep in the bottom drawer of a chest of drawers all wrapped up in a blanket. We hardly saw our older brothers, Mickey, Johnny and Stevie, as they were always out and about doing their thing.

My brother Mickey was the boss man, as he was the eldest. Then there was Johnny, who was the strong, quiet type, followed by Stevie, who would always be out of the house either working or looking for work. The three of them were at an age where they were out and about most of the time. I remember the first time that Johnny brought his girlfriend to our house. She was an attractive girl by the name of Theresa (Johnny and Theresa went on to marry and raise a family together).

I remember coming in from the street one day crying as someone had hit me. I went into the kitchen and Theresa sat me on her knee and consoled me while Johnny had gone to use the toilet that was obviously outside in those days. I can picture her now: she had lovely auburn hair and striking looks, and she was very kind. When Johnny came back in from the toilet, he clipped me around the ear and sent me back out to play. Our Mickey, who was the eldest of the siblings, was courting a beautiful girl called Nancy Mooney (Nancy and Mickey would also go on to marry and to have a family together). Nancy was one of the kindest people I have met in my life.

Chapter Five

Turmoil

One day, whilst we were playing out in a nearby street, Mill Street, our sister Edie found us and said, "You need to come home straight away. It's very important. Dad sent me to get you all in."

Sure enough, it was very important, and it was a day that changed all of our lives forever. I remember seeing my dad in the front room, the priest, the doctor and what seemed to be almost the entire street. We could not move in the house for people. Our beloved mother, a mother of 12 children, had sadly died aged just 39 from tuberculosis, which was common in those days. Our family was devastated. I recall seeing our youngest sister, Kathleen, who was a newborn baby, being cradled in the arms of my eldest sister Edie. The tears flowed.

Our mother's funeral took place in St James Church and we all had new clothes to wear for this day that I never dreamed I would see. I had never had new clothes before, and was given a new black jumper, grey trousers and a pair of black shoes. I didn't know where these new clothes had come from, but Mother would have wanted us all to look Smart, I am sure. Our dear mother was laid to rest in Ford Cemetery. Little did I know of the turmoil that lay ahead in my life.

Dad struggled to cope with all of us kids and he also became very ill himself. I did not know until a lot later in life, but tuberculosis had struck again. One day, two big black cars pulled up outside our house. In no time at all, Paddy, Alec and myself were bundled into one of the cars and Edie, Mary, Aggie and the babies (Kathleen and Richie) were piled into the other and off we went in our separate directions to begin our journeys of sorrow and despair.

It had been reluctantly agreed that we would be taken into care until Dad was well enough to return from hospital to look after us. Paddy was nine years old, Alec was five and I was seven. We were totally unaware of what was going on at the time – all we knew was that these cars had turned up from nowhere and we had been taken away from our family by strangers. Terrified, confused and angry, we did not know what was going on or what lay ahead of us.

The black car that Paddy, Alec and I were in took us to a Roman Catholic orphanage called Nazareth House, which was in Ditton, near Widnes. We did not have a clue where we were. I remember clinging tightly to Paddy and Alec on our journey to the orphanage whilst we all cried our eyes out. Upon our arrival, the nuns took the three of us to the kitchen and gave us some food. They then showered us and gave us new clothes to put on. They showed us where our beds were, in a large, cold room that was shared by what seemed to be dozens of other children.

The nuns were strict, and our Paddy soon got moved on to a different part of the orphanage. I am not sure if he was separated from us because he was that little bit older than us or because perhaps he refused to conform and accept his new surroundings. The latter was quite likely. Either way, Alec and I did not see Paddy for quite some time. This left us feeling more alone than ever. Alec and I spent most of our time without Paddy hugging each other and sobbing. One day, quite a few weeks later, Alec and I, accompanied by one of the nuns, were walking down the corridor in Nazareth House.

All of a sudden, the lone figure of a child appeared and stood at the end of the corridor near the doors. It was our brother Paddy, at long last. Paddy stood there as if he meant business, and both Alec and I raised a smile from ear to ear when we saw our big brother after what seemed to have been a very long time.

"What are you doing here, Patrick?" the sister yelled at our Paddy.

"I'm taking them home," replied Paddy.

"Who?" Sister said.

"Alec and Tommy. They're coming home with me now," Paddy went on to shout angrily.

"Oh no they're not, Patrick," said the sister as she pushed past Paddy and continued to block the doors to prevent the escape.

In a flash, Paddy picked up a chair and smashed the nun over the head with it in an attempt to escape and take us home to Bootle. Within seconds, there were nuns running down the corridor to the scene, a couple of whom grabbed Alec and I. However, Paddy gave them the slip and ran as fast as he could through the doors and away. He knew he would be getting lashed with the leather belt by the nuns if they caught him (Paddy carried the scars on his back as a result of such violent lashings he gained at the various establishments of the system for the rest of his life.) This was our first escape attempt – instigated by our Paddy to get back to the family we hoped we would one day see again. I will never forget that moment when Paddy came to take us home,. It showed the love he had for his brothers and his courage.

Some time passed by and one day we were called into the office of the sister in charge and we were told that we were to be going home. We were so happy to be leaving the orphanage and to be going home to Dad and the rest of the family. Dad was out of hospital now, and we arrived home to 1a Holywell Road to find us all together again, except for the two youngest siblings, Kathleen and Richie. At the time, I did not know where they had gone and if I would ever see them again.

Chapter Six

Home Again

Dad was no longer able to work. He continued to visit his mother in Derby Road most days, and he would come home in the evening. Looking back, I am not sure if Dad was going there for a rest, as he may not have been well still. This left Edie, Mary, Aggie, Mickey, Johnny and Stevie to look after the family. Now, having a little more freedom, we naturally began to venture further afield for our amusement and fun. We started spending more time down on the Dock Road, as there was so much going on down at the docks and so much more mischief to be had as a result. Ships from all over the world would use the port of Liverpool and sailors from every country you can imagine and they would frequent the local pubs when their ships were docked.

Most of these sailors would be smoking cigarettes, and they would discard a wide range of variety of cigarette boxes on the Dock Road. As children, we would pick these cigarette packets up off the floor with the hope of collecting the foreign cigarette cards. We would have a competition to see who could collect the most cards. In those days, nobody knew of the dangers of cigarettes and some of the children, including our Paddy and Siddy McKevitt, would light and smoke the odd discarded one out of curiosity.

We would also walk from our house down Derby Road and down on to the Dock Road which would take us through Seaforth and up to the Pierhead in Liverpool. It was probably about six miles. Our little group would often walk this route, and we would ask the sailors for cigarette cards as we passed every dock on the way. The trams, which were powered by electricity, used to run along that route. This added to the fun we could have on the way. The driver and his mate would have a large pole which they would use to lift the overhead electric cables back on to the tram if they came out of their runners, but these poles also had another use.

As the tram passed, we would jump onto the front bumper to hitch a ride, much to the annoyance of the driver and his mate. They would use these large poles to try and poke and hit us off their tram, but more often than not, we would position ourselves just that little bit out of reach. It annoyed them, but made us laugh. They couldn't stop the tram to get us off, as it would take ages to stop the machine, by which time we would have been on our toes and away. They also had a tight schedule to stick to, so this meant we were literally in the driving seat.

The Pierhead was also a great place for us to have fun. The ferry to Birkenhead used to leave from there, so we used to sneak on the boat regularly. We would hide under the gangplank until the tide came in as the gangplank would be raised by the water when the tide rose. When the boat was moored and the gangplank was at the right height, we would bunk onto the boat and enjoy the trips across the River Mersey. We were in our element feeding the seagulls with any pieces of bread that passengers may have left. When the ferry came into dock, we would quickly hide under the lifeboats to ensure we didn't get caught. We spent days doing this and enjoyed every minute of it. After a long day at sea, we would then walk all the way home to Bootle before it got dark and our elders would be out looking for us.

Another popular pastime and interest was pigeons. Everybody seemed to be pigeon mad in those days, and the majority of the men would have pigeon lofts in their yards to house their racing birds. We were one of the few houses in the street that didn't have a pigeon loft, as my dad was not keen on them. Dad used to call pigeons flying rats. Most of our mates' fathers kept pigeons and we would spend ages looking at them. We were convinced that if we caught a saddleback bird and took it home, then our dad would be converted. A saddleback was either a white pigeon with a black patch on its back or a black bird with a white patch on its back. They were quite rare and sought after in the pigeon-following community. After being shown how to make a snare to catch a bird, Paddy, Alec, myself and Siddy McKevitt decided to go on a hunt to catch one.

Along the Dock Road, where all the horses and carts would be parked up outside the dock gate waiting to take their loads in or to collect a new one, we would sneak up on the horse from behind and would yank some hair from its tail. You can imagine the surprise for the the driver when the horse kicked out and the cart would often go up in the air as a result of our military-like manoeuvre. There would be shouting and balling from the driver and general chaos would unfold as we would run off as fast as we could to avoid getting caught. The horsehair would be used to make the noose to snare a pigeon.

A loop would be made out of the horse hair and we would get a piece of old iron, such as a bolt or a small weight from the coal yard, and attach the noose to it. We would then carefully lay out the rest of the hair along the floor, cover it with horse manure and straw, and put corn over the top of it, leading to the noose. Sure enough, the pigeons would soon come down and they would be happily pecking away at the corn until eventually, one of them would put their head through the loop whilst munching its free meal and the noose would tighten with the weight of the metal as it went to move off.

The other pigeons would fly off, leaving one poor bird trapped in our snare. If the pigeon was any good, then we kept it and would give it to a family on our street to eat in a pie, but if they weren't any good, then they got necked (choked). We spent hours and hours making these snares, and if we caught a pigeon that we thought looked like a healthy bird, then we would take them to a man on the street, who would keep it. He would take its flight feathers out and keep it in his loft. There was a tale that some of the lads who caught pigeons used to sell them to the Chinese families in the area for food.

There was a competition between the little gangs of kids in our area to see who could catch the most pigeons in a week. Every street had its own little gang, and to be in one, then you had to be worthy of your membership. These gangs of kids were not like those of today – they did not really fight with each other, and the term merely meant the groups of friends who simply hung around together and played together at the time. Holywell Road did not have its own gang, as we were all part of Rhyl Street's gang.

The Rhyl Street gang did everything together. As we got older, our chosen playground progressed from the streets of Bootle to the railway or 'The Ralla', as it was affectionately known. We would play on the railway lines, and our activities in the summer included chasing butterflies and birds down the tracks to try to get the nicest-looking creatures to take home to show off.

To become a fully-fledged member of the Rhyl Street gang, there was a three-part initiation process, which involved the railway. The first stage of the initiation process involved the goods yard track that passed through the back of Marsh Lane and Brook Road. The track was used to transport goods from the docks into the city, and this part featured high rails, which gave the carriages a little more ground clearance than the conventional track. It was a very busy railway line. The initiation into the Rhyl Street gang was scary, to say the least. You had to get into this hole that we had dug between the railway sleepers in the middle of the rail track and lie there as the train went over the top of you. Seeing a train literally drive over you and feeling the wind from its passing was a terrifying experience. Looking back, it was a stupid thing to do.

There was also a tunnel on the railway nearby that we used to call the 'Half Miler', as that was supposedly the length of the tunnel through which the trains would travel up from the docks and off to Manchester.

Any new member would have to lie down on the track and put their ear to the rail to listen for the noise of the train coming down the track. Once the train close, the individual would then have to run as fast as they could to try to make it through the pitch-black tunnel before getting caught and potentially hit by the train. Inside the tunnel, there were two places we used to call the 'lookouts'. Here, you could stand in what were like sentry boxes cut into the walls of the tunnel for the workmen to take cover in safety while the train passed.

The train would literally speed past just inches from you, and it was terrifying every time. Once you had reached these lookouts, you would have to decide whether to chance your luck and continue on the second half of the tunnel before the train caught you. If you stopped and hid from the train in a lookout, then the initiation would not be complete and you would have to try to try again until you had successfully run through the entire tunnel in one hit before the train caught you.

The third and final stage of the Rhyl Street Gang's railway-based initiation processes involved the footbridge that spanned the railway between Bootle Station and across to Stanley Road. To be in the gang, you had to walk over the bridge whilst balancing on the handrail, which was about four inches wide. To help you along with the challenge, you would have an umbrella, as we thought that this would help to slow your fall if you were unlucky enough to fall off to your right hand side below to the railway tracks. If you were going to fall off, then falling to the safety of the footpath and steps to your left was the best move. It did not always work out that way, though.

One day, a friend of ours called Matthew Brady (Matty), was undertaking this particular challenge and whilst balancing on the top of the railway bridge handrail, he slipped off and fell to his right. This unfortunate incident disproved our theory of the umbrella parachute, and poor old Matthew crashed to the floor like a ton of bricks. Matty laid on the rail track like a mashed-up string puppet as we all rushed to get him off the tracks and put him on the bank at the side before a train came and finished him off. One of our group ran to tell someone at the railway station to call for an ambulance for Matty. We hid close by, so we could watch over him until the ambulance arrived. Matty broke both of his legs and was in a right state for quite some time. After this, Matty Brady was an honorary member of the Rhyl Street gang. Much to his relief, he did not have to go back and complete the challenge.

The railway in the summer months also provided us with a valuable source of coal. Our group would stand on the track in front of the oncoming trains, and the stokers at the front of the steam engine would throw lumps of coal at us in an attempt to get us off the track and away from the train. We would walk for miles up and down the track making a nuisance of ourselves, and we would then collect all the coal that had been thrown at us earlier and we would take it in turns to take it home to use as fuel for a fire. Coal was a luxury, and assuming the hunter-gatherer role, we would often return from our railway adventures with a treasure of coal. The Stokers had a hosepipe that was their preferred method of crowd dispersal; only it was not water that came out of this hose pipe, but red hot steam. Obviously, we tried to avoid getting hit as best we could.

There was a British Rail yard down the Docks Road that had four railway tracks on which the open-topped carts would pull in to get unloaded into the lorries to be taken to the docks. There was also a very large shed at this yard, the roof of which had become a large nesting ground for hundreds of pigeons. I remember, on numerous occasions, sneaking into the shed with Alec and scaling a ladder to get inside the large clock on what we called the tower.

It was here that we would hide until the railway workers had clocked off and gone home. We would then bravely crawl across the steel beams in the roof to get to the pigeon nests. The beams were about six inches wide and about 25 feet above the ground, but this didn't stop us in our quest to get the young pigeons, or squeakers, as we used to call them. Alec and I would then stick the young birds up our jumpers and carefully climb down and take the birds to the houses, of some of our friends as our dad was not a fan of pigeons, and would have never have allowed us to bring them home to Holywell Road.

Alec and I soon agreed that we would unofficially convert the three rooms at the top of our house – the attic, as we called it, into our very own secret pigeon loft without anyone knowing. The only time we really went up there was to watch the docks on fire after a bombing raid during the war. Alec and I smuggled in some old orange boxes, put some wire mesh in the front of the boxes, and soon we had a few squeakers in there.

The pigeons we had taken home were very young, so Alec and I would have to chew the corn that we had borrowed from the docks and then let them take it from our mouths. This went on for a few weeks, and the birds soon grew and they became used to us. Within a month or so, the pigeons had grown enough to be let out to fly away, so one day we opened the windows of the attic to let them get out, only to find that the birds kept returning to the house, as if it was now their permanent home. This was not in our original plan.

One day, our dad looked up to the top of the house on his way home from work, to see these pigeons flying in and out of the house.

"Paddy, what are those birds doing flying in and out of our house?" he said, thinking that Paddy may have been up to something.

"I don't know, Dad," said Paddy.

"Well, you better get up there and take a look," Dad told him. Paddy reported back and said, "Dad, Alec and Tommy are keeping pigeons up in the attic."

Dad made us bring all the boxes of birds down at once, and he took them over to Georgie McKevitt's house, as Georgie used to breed pigeons at the time. That was the end of Tommy and Alec's pigeon farm at 1a Holywell Road. It was fun while it lasted.

Chapter Seven

Day to Day

As I say, times were hard and after Mother had passed away, Dad was spending more time at home and less time at work on the docks. He would always wear a suit at the weekends, as many men did then. Mary and Edie would have to take this suit down to the local pawnshop every Monday morning to get enough money to buy food for the family for the week ahead. Dad would go back to the pawnshop on a Friday and repay the money he had lent against the suit, and get it back out for the weekend. We got to know the local pawnshop very well over time. Most families seemed to be pawning something or other on a weekly basis just to make ends meet.

Besides us kids gathering coal from the railway, the main source of fuel came as a result of an initiative by the local authority, whereby once a month families would be entitled to go to the gasworks and collect a hundred weight of coke (a form of coal). We had to supply our own sacks, but living just off the busy docks meant that such sacks were never scarce. Edie, Mary and Paddy would take the pram all the way up Marsh Lane and queue up outside the gasworks. When it was their turn, they would take the pram inside and Paddy would shovel a hundred weight of coke into the sack and they would wheel it back home. The pram would then have to be scrubbed clean again by one of the girls.

My mother had grown up on Marsh Lane, and the road featured many shops that were all busy at the time. They all remembered my mother, and they all had pleasant things to say about her. One of these shops that sticks in my mind was a bakery called Blackledges that was situated at the top of Chestnut Grove. We would go in there and one of the women would kindly give us a bag of broken biscuits for us to take home for something to eat. One of my dad's friends worked in Hawtons Coal Yard and he would always throw an extra bag of coal on his lorry and drop around to our house if he was delivering in our street. In my eyes, both the bakery and the coal yard were very good to our family, and we all appreciated their kindness.

There was a pub at the end of our street, and we would often see the men outside the pub playing a game called Pitch and Toss, whereby they would throw money up against a wall and if the coins came down heads up, then they would win and tails up, they would lose. This game was illegal at the time, so the men would pay us kids to keep lookout for police officers. Our little gang would split up and stand at each end of the lane and keep a look out for the bizzies, and if they did come, we would whistle to alert the men and they would all scatter back in to the pub before they got caught. Our lookout services were also employed by the local bookmaker, Joe Cunningham, (or Joe Cunny, as he was fondly known), as his trade was also deemed illegal at the time. Joe Cunny would stand in the jigger taking bets off everyone on horse and dog racing, and he would employ us to stand guard and warn him of the arrival of any police officers.

Another favourite pastime of ours was what called taking a legger. This involved us waiting at the traffic lights for a lorry to pull up and then jumping on to the back of it, out of the sight of the driver. We would hang onto the back of the lorry until we arrived at a stop at another set of traffic lights or until we had been bubbled and caught. One of the best lorries to do this on was the Tate and Lyle lorry, which would regularly pass by carrying sugar from the docks. Alec and I would jump onto the back of the lorry and fill our little paper bags full of sugar, having carefully torn open the big brown sacks of the sugar cargo. We would scoff some of it on our way home and take the rest back for the family to use. It was great fun.

I remember one day, as we were taking a ride on the back of a lorry, looking back and seeing a big black police car following us. At the next set of traffic lights that switched to red, the bobbies jumped out of their car and grabbed Alec and I and took us home to our house. They knew who we were and where we lived. "Dick, we found these kids of yours hanging on the back of a lorry, so we've brought them home to you," said one of the police officers as Dad opened the door to the house.

"Get in here now, you two, and get upstairs to your room," Dad snarled.

Dad made a cup of tea for the bobbies, which they drank as they all chatted about our actions. Alec and

I knew what was coming once the bobbies had left, and that would be the leather belt again.

At one time, the Boy Scouts Brigade decided that it would build a Scout hut and open a branch on Denby Street near Marsh Lane. The hut was built and the doors of the Denby Street Boy Scouts Brigade were open to recruit new members from the surrounding streets.

News of this travelled and our group of mates from Holywell Road and Rhyl Street went down with the intention of joining and having some fun as Boy Scouts. Anyway, for some reason or other, we were all turned away and were told that we were not allowed to join. We left there dejected and annoyed that we were not considered suitable to join. A few days, later the new hut was mysteriously burned to the ground, and that was the end of the Denby Street branch of the Boy Scouts Brigade.

As children we would often wander, in the search of excitement and amusement, down to the Seaforth Docks, where most of the Norwegian Sailors came in. They would drink at a large pub on the corner called The Caradock. To get to the Caradock, we had to walk down what was known as the Cinder Path, which was a path alongside the railway line running from Bootle along to Seaforth. There was a certain gang who we called the Cinder Path Gang who would hang out on this path.

They were quite a bit older than we were, and there was always more of them than there was of us. If they caught any of us Bootle Bucks (as kids from the Bootle area were often known) walking down their path, then they would chase us, catch us and give us a few digs; so we were always on red alert looking out for them when we ventured through their precious pathway.

The only escape route from the Cinder Path Gang if they appeared was to jump onto the railway and cross the electric lines – again, a silly thing to do, I know, but as kids, we had very little fear or idea of danger. When it came to the crunch and to avoid a battle with the odds stacked against us, we would leg it down the bank and dance across the railway lines, shouting abuse at them in our escape. This only made their determination to give us a hiding stronger for the next time we ran the gauntlet of the Cinder Path.

I remember my eldest sister, Edie, had got herself a job at a canteen down on the Dock Road. I remember her getting all dressed up to go to work on her first day. With her hair combed, ribbon in her hair and lipstick and make-up applied, she was ready to go. Ready to go, that was, until Dad saw her and told her that she wasn't leaving the house looking like that. He made her remove all make-up before she was allowed out of the house. I remember that when my mother was alive, my dad also prohibited her from wearing make-up.

Edie started her new job, and she enjoyed it. She would leave the house in the morning, work a full day at the canteen and then come home in the early evening. This meant that Dad had to muck in with us kids and do more housework than he was doing before, as Edie had always been the main house cleaner until she got her job.

The job gave Edie a sense of freedom and she was glad to get out to work. It was not long before she began seeing a guy called Ronnie Edwards, whom she eventually married some years later. I remember Ronnie coming to the house one day to introduce himself to Dad and to take Edie out. The door opened and there was a smart-looking man who was dressed in a fashionable two-tone overcoat, and brown shoes with white toecaps on them. Dad went to the door and asked who he was, and Ronnie replied, "Hello. I'm Ronnie, Edie's boyfriend."

"Boyfriend? You'd better clear off from here now if I were you," Dad growled back at him.

We heard Dad raise his voice at Ronnie as he continued to take his jacket off, ready to give Ronnie a hiding. Before Dad got his jacket off, Ronnie had done the sensible thing and was last seen running down the street, brown spats and all, into the distance. That was the first and last time Ronnie came to our house.

As you can imagine, there were never many boys calling to the house for our sisters. I do, however, remember an evening when Alec and I were up to our usual trick of sticking our heads through the banisters at the top of the stairs to nose at what was going on downstairs. Anyway, this particular evening we saw our sister Mary saying goodnight to a soldier who had obviously had more success in passing the gatekeeper than Ronnie Edwards did previously.

This soldier was in uniform with his beret tucked neatly onto his shoulder strap. Alec and I watched from our lookout point and as they said goodnight, this soldier leant forward and kissed our sister Mary. Both Alec and

I thought it would be hilarious to try to get Mary in trouble with Dad for kissing this bloke and we shouted, "Dad, Dad, there's a soldier in the hallway kissing our Mary."

My sister Mary was not happy, as we had obviously spoilt her moment of romance with her boyfriend. She quickly shouted up to Alec and I, and we legged it back to bed in a fit of giggles. We later got to meet this soldier, whose name was Norman Yardley. He was a lovely man who treated our Mary and all of us very well indeed. Mary went on to marry Norman some years later, and they spent the rest of their days together raising a family of their own.

My brother Stevie also had a job. He used to drive lorries for a local timber yard, and I remember one day he came home with a full-sized table tennis table, which found a home in our attic. Alec and I were chuffed and spent hours playing table tennis with our Stevie in the attic after he had finished his shifts. Stevie did his best to try to keep us occupied and off the streets and out of mischief whenever he could. Stevie knew Dad was struggling to look after us, as he was himself unwell, although us younger children were unaware of this at the time.

Chapter Eight

The Terrible Twins

Paddy would have the occasional game of table tennis with us, but he seemed to spend all of his time down at the boxing club. Paddy really loved his boxing and was making great progress – he was a formidable opponent in his many amateur fights. Paddy took his boxing seriously, and would train hard. He would go running for miles and his boxing trophies seemed to be coming in thick and fast. Paddy soon became the North of England Champion and he reached the finals of the ABA Final (the Amateur Boxing Association Final was the UK Final of the competition between all amateur boxers) twice – but on both occasions, he was not allowed to fight, as he had failed his pre-fight medical.

Paddy failed the medical on the grounds of being too light to fight in his weight category. He even resorted to having two hands full of the old-fashioned pennies to try to tip the scales in his favour at the weigh-in. On both occasions that he reached the final, Paddy would have fought opponents that he had previously beaten in club bouts. He was devastated at not being allowed to fight for and possibly win the title of ABA champion. Paddy did not really box much after that, and his talent was wasted. He had a large number of boxing bouts, and his opponents rarely went the distance!

At one point, an American man called Al Weill, the trainer of Rocky Marciano, who was the heavyweight world champion at the time, paid a visit to the gym that Paddy frequented. He had heard of two rising stars in the gym: Paddy Porter and a guy called David Rent, and he had monitored their progress from afar. Al Weill spoke to Paddy and offered him the chance to go back to America with him, where he would train and nurture him into a true professional. He said that he felt like Paddy had the potential to definitely reach the top 10 in the world at welterweight. Paddy politely declined Al Weill's offer, as he felt that he could not leave his family. David Rent went on to become an established and successful professional fighter. Our Paddy was a true champion in my eyes.

Bonfire Night in our area was a night all the local children looked forward to. Each street would have its own bonfire on a patch of wasteland where a house once stood before the German bombers had destroyed it in the Blitz. The children would go around collecting timber from anywhere they could, and the kids of each street became proud and somewhat protective of their bonfire. As the big day grew closer and the bonfires were stacked higher and higher, the chances of a rival gang setting fire to our bonfire increased dramatically – so much so that kids would have to take turns guarding the bonfire around the clock.

Some of the older kids, who were allowed to stay out later than we were, would even sit in the centre of the bonfire late into the night to prevent a rogue attack from a rival gang. We used to take pride in sneaking around to another street's bonfire and putting a match to their bonnie before Bonfire Night and we would then brag that our street had the only bonfire in the area. Everything that was wooden and removable, from old chairs to stolen toilet seats from people's outside toilets, would be added to our bonfire in a final push to build the best bonfire in the area. The pride of our street was at stake here. Our firework display on the night consisted of a few penny bangers, and we were quite content with just watching our bonfire blazing away whilst we saw the sky illuminated with the fireworks from other displays.

Learning to ride a bike is a memorable stage in the life and times of any child growing up. As children, we never had bikes, as our family could not afford to buy one, but this did not stop us. Alec, myself and Paddy would either borrow or acquire a bike, albeit it would more often than not be a bike that was intended to be used by an adult, as opposed to a little person. It made mastering this art more difficult, but we all did it.

I can see Alec now, crouching under the crossbar on a full-sized man's bike that we had temporarily borrowed from the Dock Road and pedalling like mad with his arms reaching up to the handlebars. His technique looked a little odd, but it was effective. He was too little to sit on the seat of the bike and to ride it in the conventional way. We all had a few crashes along the way, as children do when they are learning to ride a bike.

Our local swimming baths were on Barrier Road, but as always in those days, we never had the money to go in, like some of the other kids did. As a result, our swimming baths was our local canal. It was here that Alec and myself learnt to swim. I must confess that our swimming baths may not have been as posh as those on Barrier Road, as the canal was full of rats and sunken barges and various objects that had found their way into the water.

One summer's day when Alec and I were happily sitting on the bank of the canal, dipping our feet in the water whilst chatting and enjoying the sunshine, when around the corner came the terrible twins. I remember bragging to them that both Alec and I could now swim, and giving Paddy some stick over the fact that he could not. Big mistake. Paddy thought that it would be a good idea to test our swimming abilities, so he threw us both in the canal. After much splashing about and spitting out of dirty canal water, we went on to our very own version of the doggy paddle across the width of the canal and back, where the terrible twins pulled us out of the water and back on to dry land and we sat and dried our clothes out in the sun.

We loved it by the canal, as it was a place where we could get away from all the hustle and bustle of the industrial dock area, and quite often we would just sit and watch the giant shire horses, dressed in their brass harnesses and finery, pulling the barges along the towpath. I loved horses and was totally fascinated. There would be a man on the back of the barge steering it along the waterway, and the giant, muscular horse would be walking along pulling their cargo down the waterways with apparent ease. The creatures were so big that they dominated the towpath. We would have to clamber up the grass verge to make space to let them pass. I thought it was amazing the way the man on the barge would shout commands to the horse, which would fully understand and obey instantly. How could one man tame such a beast of an animal?

Another fond memory that sticks in my mind is in the summer, when the fairground would come to the North Park, at the top of Marsh Lane where it joined Strand Road. The park was huge, with numerous football fields, a duck pond and swings. Once we had got our bearings we had great fun and could often be found there playing in the summer evenings. The fairground would come and set up in North Park every year. It brought many fairground rides and a large tent where men would challenge a prizefighter for money.

People would pay to go into this tent and a challenger from the crowd would be sought for an opportunity to fight the fairground's very own champion. Whoever won got some prize money. As you can imagine, there were also side bets galore going on. There were no judges, no rounds, and the two fighters would stand there and fight with boxing gloves on until one of them either dropped or was dropped. Some of these fairground men were as rough and tough as they came, and their champion would hardly ever come unstuck. Children were not allowed into this tent, as it was a men-only affair.

I remember one year when curiosity got the better of Alec, myself and Paddy and we covertly crawled under the canvas at the back of the tent to watch the guys fighting. When we got in there, we saw the fairground champion prize fighter – quite a big man, who looked strong as an ox – sitting in the one corner all gloved up and ready to fight. There was also the ringmaster, shouting to invite anyone to step up to and fight their champion for the prize. We were shocked when our older brothers, Johnny and Mickey, stood up and accepted the challenge before climbing into the boxing ring. There were cheers for Johnny from all the men from Marsh Lane, who were in the tent.

Our Johnny stripped to the waist and stood there in his trousers and shoes with his lean and muscular physique, and got gloved up, ready for action. We had never seen Johnny fight with gloves on before, but we knew that he was a tough man who could fight well, so we sat and watched intently as the bell went and the fighting began. The fairground champion was built like a brick toilet,. He had hands like shovels and a neck like a leg.

The bout was a gruelling one that left the fairground champion on this occasion somewhat shocked. Johnny battered his opponent all round the ring until he finally stopped the brute after what must have seemed like an eternity of fighting. Mickey and all the guys from the lane celebrated Johnny's victory and we joined in the celebrations from our secret watching point until we got caught and thrown out again. We were all proud of Johnny when he stepped up to dethrone the prize fighting champion in such a convincing way.

There was a pub on Marsh Lane, which is still there today, called The Salisbury Hotel or 'The Sollie' as it was known, and this was the pub my older brothers would frequent as their local. The Salisbury Hotel at the time had a very good football team. Johnny played centre forward for them and again, he excelled. By all accounts, Johnny was one of the best players that had ever played in that league and definitely good enough to have turned professional in his day. My other brother, Stevie, played in goal for the team and was very good indeed. Rumour has it that Wolverhampton Wanderers FC were interested in signing Stevie when he was a teenager, but my dad, being a staunch Liverpudlian, would not allow Stevie to accept their offer.

The Salisbury Hotel football club is still running to this day. In fact, one of Stevie's sons, Ian, is running it and people still talk about the team when Stevie played in goal and Johnny up front today. The team won every trophy that was going at the time. I am a devoted Evertonian and the only time that I have ever set foot in Anfield (the home of our red neighbours and footballing rivals, Liverpool FC) was to watch Stevie and Johnny play for the Sollie's team in the final of the Liverpool Cup. The Sollie won, and I have never set foot in the ground again!

The two Porter and Nolan families did not get on. After our parents died, my mother was buried in the Nolan family grave in Ford Cemetery and my dad was buried some 300 yards away in the Porter family grave. I found this out when I was trying to trace my family history some years ago and when I asked my older brothers and sisters why this was the case, I never got an answer. Photographs of my parents are rare. I have a photograph of my father that was handed down to me by my dear sister Mary, but sadly, I have never owned a picture of my mother. I asked all the family if there was one, but apparently they have all being trying to find a photograph of her for over 50 years with no success to date.

I had heard that the picture of my dad was on his wedding day and somebody had cut my mother out of the picture, which breaks my heart. However, there is no proof of this being the case. I have spoken to many friends of the family and of my mother, who all describe her as being a quiet and lovely-looking woman. I live in hope of one day finding a picture of my mother, but until then, I will continue to remember her sitting on the front door step combing her lovely long black hair.

I do not know the exact date we came home from the orphanges the first time, but it was 1949. My sister Edie left home to get married to Ronnie Edwards in 1950, so that left Stevie, Mary and Aggie to look after Alec and I, as Paddy was always capable of looking after himself. Joan, Richie and Kathleen remained in care and I didn't see them again for quite some time (it was over forty years before I saw my sister Kathleen again, but that's another story). As kids, we never really knew what had happened to them.

Stevie and Mary would get us ready for and off to school before Stevie started work at the timber yard and Mary on the house. It was at this time that Paddy, Alec and I started to dodge school and play on the railway. We would go home and try to act as if we had been at school all day, but this did not last long, as little did we know but some of my dad's mates worked on the railways as train drivers and reported us to him. Dad was very ill at this time, and was being cared for by his mother, Granny Porter, at her house on Derby Road.

Mary left school in June of 1949 and got a job in Bells Canteen on the Dock Road. The school board had warned Stevie about our continuous absence from school, and he sat us down and made us promise to attend. We promised him that we would attend school every day as of the start of the new term after the summer holidays.

Having lost our mother in 1948 we, as a family, were totally devastated. However, our lives spiralled into further despair and sadness when in October 1952, our dad sadly died of tuberculosis. We were all totally devastated and our Paddy, in particular, was completely distraught. I remember all of us gathering at our house and walking to Granny Porter's to see our dad, but I have no recollection of seeing him. I think Granny Porter stopped us young ones from doing so as we were so upset.

On the day of my father's funeral, there was a large crowd of people at Granny Porter's house, including relatives and friends of the family who all came to pay their respects to my dad. I hardly knew any of them, as there were so many people there. To this day, I can picture the fleet of big black funeral cars, one of which carried us kids, driving down Derby Road on to Millers Bridge. There were hundreds of people lining the streets, standing on the pavements, and all the men took off their flat caps and the women blessed themselves as Dad's coffin passed by the Old Toll Bar Pub. The funeral procession went to St James Church on Marsh Lane, where a mass took place to celebrate and remember the life of my father. We left the church with Dad's coffin and made our way to Ford Cemetery where we laid hin to rest. That was one of the last days I spent in Bootle as a lad.

Chapter Nine

Bamber Bridge

Dad died in the October, and it was coming up to Christmas when our brother Stevie called Alec and I into the front room of our house and sat us down to break some bad news. He told us that he had tried his very best to keep the family together and to make sure we all stayed together, but he could no longer look after us, and that the authorities had thought it was in our interest to place Alec and I in the care of an orphanage. Paddy had really struggled with losing Dad, and by this time, he had been taken away and placed in approved school (a detention centre) due to him going off the rails and getting in trouble with the police after Dad died. Aggie had gone to live with our sister Edie in North Wales, where her husband was from.

Although we were very upset, we knew that Stevie had done his best to look after us and to run the house whilst juggling a job that provided a much-needed source of income. As we all sat there in our front room crying and awaiting the inevitable separation from what we had left of a family, a big black, official-looking car pulled up outside the house. Alec and I were put into this car and we were taken away from Bootle. Our hearts broke as we sat in the back of this car hugging each other tightly and watching our beloved dog, Lady, running behind the car until we lost sight of her. We loved that dog, as she had gone everywhere with us, and we never saw her again. The dog seemed to chase the car for ages, and we gave up all hope of staying in Bootle when she faded into the distance.

Both Alec and I were on a mystery trip of fear again and travelled into the darkness to our unknown destination. We were upset and scared, but at least we had each other. It was dark when we arrived at Bamber Bridge, which was a children's home based some 30 miles away from Bootle, near Preston. Obviously, Alec and I did not know this at the time – we just knew that we had been taken away from our family and had no idea what was going to happen to us next. The car pulled up outside this building and we were met by a man and a woman, who then took us both to a large kitchen area and gave us some food. We were very hungry by that time, and must have looked like proper little urchins in need of help.

Later that evening, once we had finished eating, we were given pyjamas to wear for bed. This was a novelty for Alec and I, as we had never worn pyjamas before. We were shown to a room that contained two single beds, and we were left alone for the remainder of the night. Only one bed was used, as we always slept in the same bed at home and we both felt like we needed to be together more than ever on this particular night. We did not get much sleep, as we were both crying continuously. Alec kept asking me, "When are we going

Home, Tommy?" and I would reply, "Don't cry Alec. Paddy will soon come and take us home." Oh, how we longed for the door to open and to see our brother Paddy appear to rescue us from this place. The door did not open, Paddy did not appear on a rescue mission and our long stay at Bamber Bridge Children's Home had begun.

The next morning, the man and the woman came to our room again and this time introduced themselves as Dr Andrews and his wife, Mrs Andrews. They explained that they would be taking care of us for the next few months until it was decided where we would go to live. Dr Andrews took us off to another room, where he gave us some new clothes to put on and then showed us to the bathroom. He told us to take a bath and put our pyjamas into a basket to be washed. Mrs Andrews filled the bath with warm water and told me to bathe myself and that she would change the bath water for Alec once I had finished. She let Alec stay in the room with me whilst I took a bath and she let me stay in the room for Alec whilst he bathed. too. This was the first time in our lives that Alec and I had seen a bath with taps on. We were amazed!

Once bathed, we both put on our new, crisp, clean clothes and off we went with Dr Andrews to the refectory, where we met the other residents of Bamber House for the first time. There were about 10 children sitting having breakfast, and Dr Andrews said to them,
"I would like to introduce Thomas and Alexander, who are from Liverpool, to you all. They will be staying with us for a while. I want you to make them feel welcome here at Bamber House."

We were then shown to our seats and ate breakfast like everyone else.

After we had finished breakfast, we were taken into an office, where Dr Andrews told us what would be happening to us, which was that we were going to be residents of Bamber House for possibly quite some time. Our hearts sank, and I asked when we could please go home, but we were simply told that, "This is your home now."

Alec and I broke our hearts crying, as we longed to go home to Bootle to our family.

One of the boys in the home was given the task of looking after us and showing us around. To be fair to him, he seemed to be pleasant, but Alec and I did not want anything to do with him or anyone. As far as we were concerned, we could trust nobody and it was me and him versus the world. We didn't interact with the group, and just stood together and watched every move they made.

Bamber House was a large property set in the countryside near Preston in the northwest of England. The doctor and his wife lived in the gatehouse, situated next to the main gates, which were substantial and made out of iron. These gates were always locked. There was a long, sweeping tree-lined driveway starting at the gates, which led to the main house, where we stayed. There was a play area to the side of the house with swings; a slide and other children's play equipment. There was also a stable and three horses there, as well as some chickens. It may well have been a farm at some time.

After we finished our tea on our first full day in Bamber House, Mrs Andrews told us that Alec would have to sleep in his own bed that night, as opposed to bunking in with me. I explained that we had always shared a bed and felt better if we were together in the nights, but she insisted that Alec slept in a separate bed. He did, but we moved our beds close together that night to make sure we were not far apart from each other. Once we had been there for a few days, Alec and I relaxed a little and got to know some of the other children some more, but not a day passed by when I didn't think of returning home to Bootle and our family.

Dr and Mrs Andrews were also teachers, and we attended the school in the home. This school was different from the one we had attended in Bootle, St James School, as it seemed fun and the teachers did not shout at us if we did not understand what they were trying to teach us during the lessons. Instead, they would take the time out to try to explain and help us understand as and when required.

In the grounds of the home ran a small stream that twisted through the nearby fields, and Alec, myself and the other children enjoyed sending twigs down the stream and pretending they were ships sailing down the River Mersey. We were never allowed anywhere near the main gates, unless we were accompanied by a member of staff. However, when I could get a glimpse of the gates and the lorries passing, I would wonder where they were going. Were they going to Bootle? Home was never far from my mind.

One day, after Alec and I had finished our breakfast, we were told that we had visitors. My heart raced and my mind wandered. Was it our Paddy coming to break us out from here, or was it another family member coming to take us both home? Alec and I skipped with anticipation behind Mrs Andrews to her husband's office, whereupon our little hearts sank again, as the visitors were not known to us. It wasn't Paddy or any of our family here to rescue us, but two strangers who wanted to ask many questions about each of us.

Our visitors looked official and began talking to Dr Andrews about us after they had finished what had felt like an interrogation. They were talking quietly, but I did overhear one of them telling Dr Andrews something that sounded like I would have to go to a Catholic school and Alec would be required to stay at Bamber House a little longer without me. That was the first time I thought of escaping as the tears rolled down my cheeks yet again.

Alec saw me crying and asked what was wrong, but I couldn't tell him what I thought I had just heard, as he would be devastated, so I just told him that I was missing Mum and Dad. There was no way I was going anywhere without my brother, I thought to myself. My mind was racing, desperately trying to hatch a plan to escape and return to Marsh Lane. I did not know how we were going to do it, but I knew that we sure as hell were going to try. I thought if we could only find our Paddy or any of the family, all would be well. We knew that Mum and Dad were dead, but there were still our brothers and sisters in Bootle, who would surely help us if we could find a way to get to them.

Early the next morning, before the sun had risen, I decided that the time was right to make a break for our freedom and to try to get back home.

"Wake up, Alec," I whispered to him as I gently tapped his hand.

"Keep quiet – we're going to make a run for it and go home to Bootle."

Alec and I put our clothes on and opened our bedroom window, being extremely careful not to wake anyone else up in the building. I climbed out on to the windowsill, lowered myself over the edge and hung on by my fingertips before dropping from the first floor into the darkness on to the ground. Alec followed closely behind me and dropped to the floor below. It was a bigger drop than I had expected, but at least we were out. I think we would have chanced the drop from any height just to avoid being separated and in an attempt to get home to find our family.

I knew that we could not go through the main gates as Dr Andrews and his wife lived in the cottage next to them, and they would surely catch us if they saw us. The gates would also be locked, so we took off and ran across the fields together under the light of the moon and fuelled on sheer adrenaline. I also knew that the alarm would be raised at 7.30 am when the staff went their daily rounds to wake the children up, so we had to get as far away as we could before that happened. We crossed the stream in the grounds at the stepping-stones and seemed to run across field after field until we came to a gate.

Alec and I dare not stop or look back; we just ran and ran until we came to a gate that led us to a cart track, which we followed for what seemed to be ages. After a while, we stopped, as we came to a house which was set back off the lane. There were three bikes leaning up against an old shed, so I whispered to Alec, "We will have these away, Alec. Let's creep up and take one each. You take the smaller one on the left and I will take the one next to it. Don't forget that we will have to get as far away as possible, Alec, before they all wake up at the home, as they will be after us once they find out we are gone."

Alec and I snuck up to the bikes, wheeled them down the lane to avoid making any noise, and jumped on them and pedalled like hell for our little lives down a lane for what seemed to be miles. We eventually came to what appeared to be a main road, and I had to make a decision with regard to which way we should continue to go. Not having a clue where we were and not being able to see any signs in the darkness, I decided we would turn left and we pedalled our getaway bikes as fast as we could along the road until we passed through a village and it started getting lighter as the sunrise broke through the darkness. We lifted our bikes over a wall and took a rest for an hour or so, as we were both worn out from what was a marathon escape effort so far.

Alec and I got back on to our bikes and continued on our quest to get home. After another couple of hours' pedalling, we reached a road sign that said Southport 10 miles. Now, I remembered that some time ago there was a trip from Holywell Street to the seaside at Southport on a charabanc (bus trip), and although none of us could afford to go on the trip, I knew that we were heading in the right direction to get home to Bootle.

This particular road was a very busy one. Lorries and cars whizzed past us, and the railway ran alongside the road, which was the other side of some sand dunes. We had ridden our bikes flat out all day, and started to get very hungry, as we had not eaten since the day before. As it started to get dark, a lorry honked its horn and the driver pulled up and got out to shout at us for not having any lights on our bikes.

"Where are you going?" asked the lorry driver.

"Home," I replied.

"Well, you'd better get home quick before the police stop you for having no lights on your bikes," he shouted.

"We only live down the road, so we will walk our bikes the rest of the way home, Mister," I answered.

The lorry pulled off and we jumped back on our bikes and continued with our epic journey home. The thought of getting caught by the police scared us, so we knew that we had to get off the main road – and quickly. We stopped at the entrance to a field, lifted our bikes over the wooden gate and walked through the field towards the railway track. As we got closer to the track, we saw an old wooden hut, so we hid our bikes in the long grass next to it and I went around to the side and smashed the small window. Alec and I climbed into the hut through the window. It was full of tools: spades, a wheelbarrow and a table and chairs. We sat there in the dark, fighting our hunger pains as we planned the next step of the escape bid. We talked late into the night and eventually fell asleep in the hut.

Suddenly, the hut shook to the point that we thought it was going to collapse around us as a train sped past early the next morning. We were awake, and the next stage of our journey home was nigh. Alec complained that he was starving and I told him that I was, too, but we couldn't really do much about that at the moment, so we'd better get moving. We cycled further down the main road until we reached a town, and it was here that we caught a glimpse of a milk cart parked up at the bottom of the drive of a posh-looking house. We could see the milkman talking with a lady at her front door, so we got off our bikes and crept up quietly to the milk cart. I swiftly took a bottle of milk and Alec got a loaf of bread before we scurried off in silence back to our bikes. We pedalled like mad with our much-needed food until we reached relative safety at the rear of a garage that was closed on the other side of town. We ate the bread and drank the milk. Oh, it tasted so good!

After more pedalling along a main road, we reached another road sign, and this one said Liverpool and All Docks, so we knew we weren't far away from home. With our spirits lifted, we pedalled some more until we saw a sign for 'Bootle and Seaforth Docks.' We passed through Formby and on to Seaforth Road, and the butterflies in our stomachs multiplied with every rotation of our pedals. Our journey continued with big smiles on our faces along the Dock Road and on to Marsh Lane. We were home at last, we thought, but we did not really know what to expect – although we surely did not expect what we saw when we eventually reached our house in Holywell Road.

Our escape mission to get home to Bootle appeared successful. However, our hearts and spirits sank when we saw that our family home was empty and boarded up.

I asked some kids who were playing out on the street – kids we didn't know – what had happened to the family that had lived in 1a Holywell Road, and they told us that they had all gone away months ago. I looked at Alec and he looked back at me. Our faces were full of disappointment and sadness, but all was not lost, as we could still go to Granny Porter's. We ditched the bikes and opted to walk to her house, so she wouldn't know that we had robbed the bikes. We thought that we could nip back and get them later if needed.

When we got to Granny Porter's house, the door was open as it always was, so Alec and I walked in to her front parlour. She looked surprised to see us, to say the least.

"Oh my God. What the hell are you two doing here?" she yelled.

"We ran away, Granny, but there is nobody at our house, so we have come to you," I told her.

"Why the hell did you run away?" she asked.

"They were going to split us up, Granny, so we ran away to stop them doing it," I replied.

Granny Porter was not alone in the house that time, as a few of our aunties were there and our Uncle Paddy was there, too. To his credit he defended us and said, "They promised that the boys would stay together."

Despite Uncle Paddy's attempt to persuade Granny Porter to let us stay, she was having none of it. Granny

Porter took us into her kitchen, made us a jam butty and gave us a hot cup of tea. Alec and I were exhausted and starving after our journey from Bamber House to Bootle.

Some time later that day, two police officers came to the house, and Alec and I knew we'd been bubbled. Before we could get on our toes again, the doors were closed and one of the police officers asked us, "Where have you run away from, boys?"

"It's a place called Bamber Bridge, but please don't send us back there, as they are going to separate me and my brother Alec," I begged.

Granny Porter chipped in and said, "Well, I can't look after them so they will have to go back to the children's home."

Alec and I were gutted. We could not understand why our very own grandmother would not take us in and let us live with her. Were we that bad? We now felt more alone and scared than ever before, as we didn't even have our brother Paddy with us to look after us anymore. Before we knew it, the police officers took hold of Alec and I, bundled us into their car outside Granny Porter's house and drove us down to the police station in Bootle Town Hall. They kindly fed us at the station before a black car again came for us and took us both back to Bamber House.

Chapter Ten

On the Move

Again we made the journey to Bamber House, both huddled together in the back of a car with the two strangers in the front. It was the same man and woman who had originally taken us from Holywell Road to the children's home. Upon arriving back at the children's home, we were met by Dr Andrews, who took us straight to the canteen and gave us some sandwiches to eat. Once we had finished eating, Alec and I accompanied Dr Andrews and these two official people who had brought us back. Many questions followed, as they obviously wanted to know the reasons why we had run away.

One of the local authority officials asked, "Have you been mistreated or abused in any way whilst you have been in the care of Bamber House? Was that the reason you both ran away, Tommy?"

"No. We ran away because the last time we were in this office with you lot, you said that I would be moving to another school and Alec would be staying here on his own," I replied whilst tears started to run down my face.

"That is not what was said, Tommy. It is the policy of social services to try to keep families together where possible, so you must have heard it wrong," the man said.

"Well, where are our other brothers and sisters, then? Where are Paddy, Ritchie, Joan and Kathleen, then? I thought you said that it was your policy to keep families together."

"Ritchie, Joan and Kathleen are being taken care of by the nuns at Nazareth House, and they are happy there," the man replied.

There was no mention of where our Paddy was. I hoped he was well.

What felt like an interrogation went on for quite some time. They also wanted to know how we managed to get back to Bootle and if anyone had helped us to do so. I simply told then that we had bunked on a train and played stupid when I was asked from which station. I did not tell them about us stealing the bikes or the bread and milk, as I was scared that we would get deeper into trouble with the police. I remembered two boys from our street who had been sent to Approved School for stealing. Looking back, I don't think anyone in the room believed my account of what happened, but I stuck to my story and Alec wisely remained silent throughout the questioning.

"You have both been very silly. You ran away to go home to your family, but your mum and dad are dead. There is nobody to look after you now, so you are to stay wherever you are sent. If you run away again, then you will be sent to a place you will never get out of. Do you understand?" the man said in a stern voice, pointing his boney finger at Alec and I.

Alec and I wept and once again felt scared and alone. There was little doubt that the man was threatening us with Approved School, and the thought of going there scared us, as we had heard bad stories about other children going there. I promised that as long as Alec and I were kept together, then we would not run away again and we would behave ourselves. After more telling off and the officials reminding us that they would be coming back to Bamber House on a regular basis to monitor our behaviour, they left us in the care of Dr Andrews again.

That night, we were taken in to the dormitory where six other boys were sleeping. I was given the bed by the door and Alec the bed furthest away from mine, at the other end of the room. It was obvious that they could easily keep a watchful eye on me if I slept there and that it would be harder for Alec and I to group together in any future escape attempts. We both eventually closed our eyes and drifted off to sleep after what had been quite an ordeal.

The next day Mrs Andrews asked me if, after school, I would like to help her feed the horses that lived in the stabled at Bamber House. I jumped at the chance and readily accepted her kind invitation, as I loved horses, and instantly cast my mind back to watching the huge shire horses pulling the barges down the canal in Bootle in those happier days when my mum and dad were alive and we all lived at home.

"Do you know anything about horses, Tommy? Have you ever been near a horse?" asked Mrs Andrews.

"No, Mrs Andrews, I haven't, but I really like horses and I would love to help you feed them. Thank you," I replied.

I dared not to tell Mrs Andrews about how we used to sneak up on the horses on the Dock Road and pull the hair out of their tales for us to make snares to catch pigeons, as I was sure she wouldn't appreciate knowing that little tidbit of information. Sure enough, after school and tea that day, I accompanied Mrs Andrews to the stables and helped out with the feeding of the resident horses. I remember having a massive grin on my face when I stroked a horse for the first time. It felt like I had not smiled for such a long time; it felt good. I was now in my element, wheeling straw in and out of the stables in the rusty old wheelbarrow. I couldn't wait to get back to see Alec and tell him about the horses.

The evening drew in and it was soon time to go to sleep in the dormitory. I slept better that night, having spent some time helping out with the horses earlier in the day, than I had done for so long. Alec seemed to have settled into the routine of sleeping on his own in the dormitory, too, so life appeared to have got a little better for us both at Bamber House. The next morning after breakfast, Dr Andrews gave me a tin box that contained all the leftover bread and toast from breakfast. He told me to go out into the field with him where the horses were and for me to bang on the tin whilst shouting the names of the horses.

"Bonny, Charlie, Prince," I yelled whilst banging the tin.

To my amazement, the three horses came galloping over to me to indulge in their breakfast treat. Dr Andrews showed me how to feed the horses with the flat of my hand.

"Don't feed them with your fingers, Tommy, or you'll end up like Alec," Dr Andrews joked.

If anyone else would have said this about Alec, then I would have taken offence, but I knew Dr Andrews was only trying to make me smile and was not being mean to Alec.

Later that morning, I told Alec about the horses and how I had been given the chance to feed them. Dr Andrews said that Alec could join me to feed the horses that evening, so we were both excited all day and looked forward to that evening. Once in the stables, I tried to persuade Alec to feed Prince, but he was having none of it. After some gentle persuasion, I managed eventually to get Alec to stroke the horse after he had plucked up the courage to do so. As Alec fed the horse, it stepped back suddenly and stepped on Alec's foot and he shouted the place down. Alec was unhurt, but the shock of it all put him right off and that was the end of his involvement with the horses at Bamber House. Alec stuck to playing football with the other children and never went near the horses again. I, on the other hand, would spend every minute I could with the horses, and I really enjoyed doing so.

A few weeks later Dr Andrews asked me if I would like to ride one of the horses. I immediately said yes. Later that day, Dr Andrews and I went to the stables, where he put a saddle on Charlie the smaller of the horses and told me to get on it. I was nervous, but excited. Here I was going to ride a horse for the first time. Once I was in the saddle, Dr Andrews led the horse out of the stables and out of the field and along a country lane. This was the most fun I had had for ages and all of my worries, fear and anger seemed to disappear for the duration of my horseback journey. Dr Andrews said that I was a natural and that I could be a jockey when I grew up. He may have been just saying this to stop me running away again, but I was now even more fascinated with horses.

Over the next few months in Bamber House, life away from our family was starting to get a little better for Alec and I. Things seemed to be settling down and we were even starting to enjoy school, not to mention I got to ride and look after horses. All was fine until one day Dr Andrews called Alec and I into his office. Upon entering Dr Andrews' office, our eyes met with the same two local authority officials who had always seemed to be bad news. I felt the colour drain from my face and felt physically sick. As my heart thumped, I immediately scanned my memory to see if we had done anything wrong but could find no reason for them to be here to see Alec and I yet again.

"You will be leaving Bamber House, as we have found a Catholic school for the two of you," said the man. "Before you ask, yes, you are being placed together," he added.

"Why can't we stay here, Sir? We are settled here and are doing well. Can we please stay here?" I begged the man.

"No, Tommy. As you are both Roman Catholics, then you both must be educated in a Roman Catholic school. Your placement here at Bamber House was only temporary," he told us in a more stern voice than previously.

Dr Andrews made it clear that we had settled down very well since their last visit and that he had had no problems with us whatsoever. Dr Andrews went on to wish us well for the future and he told us that he hoped we would continue with the good behaviour in our new school.

"We will miss you helping us with the horses Tommy. Be good," were the parting words from Dr Andrews.

Alec and I got into the car, having said our goodbyes to Dr Andrews and his wife. So that was it. We were uprooted and were on the move again.

Chapter Eleven

St. Peter's Catholic School

After quite some time in the car, it turned off a main road and pulled up outside a large iron gate. The gate guarded the tree-lined driveway that led to a red brick building that appeared a lot larger than Bamber House. Its whole appearance felt intimidating. The main building was attached to a church. Alec and I had arrived at St Peter's Catholic School. The car pulled up outside the main entrance of the building and there were two men dressed in black cassocks standing there waiting for us. If they were priests, then they did not look like friendly ones, that is for sure, judging by the way in which they glared at us both. Alec tugged my sleeve, as he often did when he was concerned or scared, so I put my arm around him and whispered, "We will be OK, mate."

The officials and the priests then took Alec and I into the building and down a long corridor. They did not speak a word to us, and we both felt uneasy, as it was becoming clearer that this was not a friendly atmosphere. As we walked down the corridor, we saw some boys who were busy cleaning the floor with their mops and buckets.

These boys stopped and stared at Alec and I as we passed them by with the priests. One of the priests shouted to the boys in an aggressive and loud voice and ordered them to get on with their work. Alec and I looked at each other, and we wished we were still at Bamber House with Dr Andrews and his wife.

We were taken into a room at the end of the corridor and we wee told to sit down beside a very long table. Alec and I listened intently to what the social services officials were saying to the priests and when they said we were from Liverpool, one of the priests muttered,

"Oh – Scousers, hey?"

I thought that was strange and had never been called that before. The door to the room swung open and in walked a rather plump looking man who was introduced as Brother John. I thought to myself, you look nothing like my brother John!

"Follow me," Brother John grumbled as he continued to walk through what seemed to be a maze of corridors and up a large wooden staircase into a room. This room featured a long table with two older boys standing behind it, almost like soldiers standing to attention. Brother John barked out a list of clothing items to the boys, who immediately searched in two rather large wooden boxes to find us appropriate uniforms. Out came short grey trousers, light blue shirts, grey jumpers, long grey socks, underpants, vests and a pair of boots each. With our uniforms held under our arms, Brother John gave us a number each and said that we must remember them. My number was 21 and Alec's was 29. Brother John went on to say that the numbers and name of the school would be sewn into our shirts and jumpers and that our coats would be issued later on that day.

"Look at that, he's got no fingers," one of the boys issuing the uniforms said as he pointed at Alec's missing fingers.

"Be quiet and get on with your work," Brother John barked back at him.

We were then escorted down the corridor to a large dormitory and were shown to our allocated beds. The room was large and there must have been 30 beds in there, arranged in three rows of ten. My bed was in the centre row and Alec's was a few beds down to my left. At least I could see Alec from my bed. I did think about asking if we could sleep in beds next to each other, but thought better of it as Brother John would have most certainly denied such a request, and I didn't want anyone to know that it bothered us being apart. I had learnt that it was not good to show weakness by letting people know what bothered you, as they would surely seize upon the opportunity to exploit it. It felt like this lot were not going to be very friendly towards Alec and I.

Brother John then called a boy in from the corridor and he introduced himself.

"Hello. I'm Patrick Rice, but everyone calls me Paddy," he said.

"Show these two where the toilets are and how they are expected to make up their beds," Brother John said firmly to the lad as he walked away.

As Paddy Rice was showing us how to make up our beds, he asked us in a quiet voice, so as not to be heard talking by the brothers, "What are your names? Where are you from and why have you been sent here?"

"I am Tommy Porter and this is my brother Alec," I replied. "Our mum and dad died and they took us away from our family and we have ended up here," I added.

Paddy Rice said that he would show us around and warned us not to answer the brothers back and to do exactly what they told us to do. Failure to do so would result in the painful punishment of receiving lashings with the cane. This confirmed my fears, and I knew that we were now in for a hard time if we dared to step out of line at St Peter's Roman Catholic School. It turned out that Paddy Rice was originally from Northern Ireland and he had been at St Peter's for two years when our paths crossed. He was a decent lad, and he showed us exactly how we were expected to make our beds up and fold our blankets to produce almost perfect corners every day.

Having made our own beds up to the required standard, and having washed and adorned ourselves in our new school uniforms, we put our old clothes into a big basket in the dormitory, and Paddy Rice took us to the dining hall, where he explained how the system of getting fed operated. I asked him if we could sit with him in the dining hall, as he was our only friend in the school, but he said that the brother who was in charge of the dining hall would decide where we sat at feeding time. Our guide showed us around the school some more and as we went to the recreation area, many boys stopped us and asked us questions. The questions mainly consisted of concerned what had happened to

Alec's fingers. At first, I told them the story of what happened to Alec and how he had lost his fingers as a result of being run over by the lorry, but the boys just laughed and ridiculed Alec. This made me angry, so I stopped telling them, which led to a little hostility from them.

The bell would ring at teatime to call all the boys to the dining hall. Each would sit in his allocated seat, which would be the same at each mealtime. The brother in charge of the dining hall told Alec and I which seats had been allocated to us, and to our relief, we were sat at the same table. We were placed at the end of the table, as it was the job of any new boy to collect the plates and cutlery and stack them on the trolley that came to collect them at the end of each mealtime.

Grace was said by everyone before meals, and each table would then have to wait for its number to be called out by the brother in charge. Once your table number had been called, you were allowed to walk in single file to the serving counter to receive whatever culinary delight was put on your plate before returning to your seat at your table.

"Come on, Porter. Get the dishes stacked ready for the trolley," shouted this lad across the dining hall as he looked at me with a big, smug grin on his face.

I collected and stacked the plates on the trolley after mealtime was over and I asked Paddy Rice who the lad shouting the orders at me was. Paddy said that the lad was the table prefect and that he was just showing you who was boss that's all, and all would be okay as long as I kept my head down and did as I was told.

Alec and I stood with our newfound friend, Paddy Rice, in the recreation hall after we had left the dining hall, observing the goings-on and the little groups that had formed in the corners. I wondered what this place had in store for Alec and I. Numerous boys came over to us and asked us questions. Some seemed to be all right, but some were obviously trying to make an impression on us and were telling us what we could or could not do and that they were in charge.

At this point, Brother John intervened and took Alec and I to show us some of the facilities, like the table tennis table. He told us that they also had a netball court and a football field in the grounds that we would be allowed to use sometimes. I think Brother John had noticed us feeling a little uncomfortable when we were surrounded by the other boys in the recreation hall, and perhaps he sensed the situation escalating if he didn't remove us from there when he did. We just stood around wand watched everyone for the first day, as our guards were up in this new environment.

The bell soon rang and it was time to go back to the dormitory to get ready to sleep. Paddy Rice had earlier tipped us off and told us that we were to stand in silence by the side of our beds and under no circumstances were we to sit or lie on the bed until the brother in charge had told us to do so. Failure to comply would result in the cane, so this top tip had firmly stuck in our minds. We followed the corridors and climbed the staircase to the dormitory that we had been shown to earlier in the day and I stood by my allocated bed and Alec by his, as did the other inmates.

A brother appeared in the doorway swishing his cane and banging it down the side of his leg. He barked orders to everyone. We all immediately stood in line for fear of receiving the cane. When all were in line, everyone knelt down by the side of the beds to pray before climbing into bed ready to sleep in what seemed to be a totally controlled and cold exercise. After this ritual was over, the brother in charge marched menacingly down to my bed with his cane in his hand and continued to lay the law down with regard to what we could or could not do at bedtime.

We were allowed to talk to each other if we kept our voices down. Raised voices were not tolerated. Leaving the dormitory was only allowed if we needed the toilet, which was situated just behind the double doors of the dormitory, which were always open. He explained that a small night-light would be left on throughout the night. At the call of lights out, everyone was expected to return to his bed and to go straight to sleep in silence. The brother then went to Alec, where he repeated the rules and regulations like a robot.

Once the brother had left the room and before lights out was called, I sat with Alec by his bed and we talked. We were both very upset, but we promised each other not to let the other boys see that we were upset, as they would think we were soft and would try to pick on us even more. Lights out was called, and I returned to my bed, but I cannot recall sleeping that much at all that night. It was times like this that I wished our brother Paddy was there with us, as we knew he would look after Alec and I. That concluded our first day at St Peter's Roman Catholic School.

The next morning I woke up startled by the sound of one of the brothers clapping his hands loudly in the dormitory.

"Wakey, wakey," he shouted in a very loud voice as he walked past each bed, ripping the sheets off each of them as he went.

Once everyone was awake and standing by the side of their bed, he carried out what was a daily inspection of the bed to see if anyone had urinated in the bed during the night. I soon found out that this wetting of the bed was common amongst the pupils of the school. This was surely related to way in which people, were treated in my opinion. This brother slammed his cane down on every bed as he passed in an attempt to stamp his dominance on the room and those within it. He was the brother in charge of the dormitories and he seemed to be a ruthless man who was not to be crossed.

After the morning bed inspection was complete and the brother in charge had flexed his ego somewhat with his position of power, we then went to the bathrooms to wash and get dressed before we were to line up by our beds again, but this time waiting for the breakfast bell. The bell rang and we made our way to the dining hall downstairs like a swarm of ants walking in single file through the well-scrubbed corridors. Alec and I sat down quietly in the seats that had been allocated to us the evening before and waited for our next instruction.

With that, the boy who had shouted at me at the dinner table the day before appeared from nowhere and put his face right in mine and said aggressively, "I am the prefect for this table and you will do what I tell you. OK?"

"Look, mate, we have just arrived here and are not looking for any trouble, so just leave us alone," I replied trying to defuse the situation.

I didn't want to get into trouble, but I wasn't going to back down from this bully, as that was not how we had been brought up. One of the brothers quickly came over to the table and told us to just get on with things and to sit down quietly. I just knew we were going to have problems with this prefect.

After breakfast, one of the brothers came to Alec and I and took us off to an office as he had said that we were going to see the abbott. The office had a large oak door with a sign saying Private. The abbott was the main man. The brother knocked on the door and took us inside the office, where we were greeted by a monk wrapped in a brown cassock with a white rope tied around his waist and he sat comfortably in a big brown leather chair by a large wooden desk. This man got out of his chair and made his way around to the front of the desk to address Alec and I.

"Have you been informed of what is expected of you here at St Peter's?" the aAbbott said in a gruff voice.

"The Father has told us where are to sleep and eat, Sir," I said, trying to please the man.

"Do not address them as Father, as they are not priests, but address them as Brother John or whatever their name may be. They are Christian Brothers," he said.

The abbott reminded us that we had to obey every instruction or order given by the brothers, or we would face punishment. As if we needed reminding. We were to attend school classes, attend church as and when required and there was to be no bullying of any of the other children in the school. The abbott went to tell us of the wide range of sporting activities available to the pupils, and he seemed pleased to hear that both Alec and I liked sports such as football, boxing and running cross country. Alec was a very good runner. He went on to say that we would each be given jobs to do in the school, such as cleaning and other work if required. We did not have any questions for him, so we were dismissed from his office, and I guess that meant we were now fully-fledged pupils of St Peter's School.

The next few days were spent trying to find out where everything was in the school and trying to get to know some of the other children. We were on our best behaviour and soon got to find out which children to stay away from, as they seemed intent on starting trouble with Alec and I. There were a few occasions when I grabbed Alec's arm and we just walked away from boys who were trying to intimidate us and start a fight. We just wanted to keep our heads down and to get through this whole ordeal and stay together.

The schoolwork was okay. I did enjoy and was good at history and reading. However, I wasn't very good at maths, and my woodworking skills left a lot to be desired. Each brother took ownership of a subject, and some would display more patience and understanding of a child's learning requirements than others. Some would give you the chance to explain why you were struggling with an answer to a certain question, whilst others would simply hit you with the cane at the first sign of you struggling. Unfortunately for the pupils at the school the first category of teaching styles was a minority.

It wasn't long until the bully-boy of a prefect crawled out from underneath his stone again in an attempt to harrass me in front of everyone. One dinner time, after we had all finished eating in the dining hall, I was carrying out my duty of gathering all the plates, associated cutlery and food waste and was placing them on to the trolley for them to be taken away for washing. As I was putting some plates on to the trolley, this prefect shoved my arm enough for all the plates to fall and smash on the floor of the dining hall. A big cheer instantly went up in the dining hall. He had succeeded in humiliating me on front of everyone – or so he thought.

I lost my temper and the red mist dawned upon me again. I smashed my fist into his mouth as hard as I could. The prefect fell to the ground and Alec and I both jumped on him and punched him repeatedly. This led to all the other boys from the table jumping on top of Alec and I and punching us over and over again. We were getting a hiding. The odds were not in our favour, and I was a little relieved when one of the brothers jumped, lashing out with his cane and shouting at the top of his voice in an attempt to quell what had almost become a large-scale disruption. The boys that had jumped on us immediately sat back down, but Alec and I kept going at it, as this prefect had to be taught a lesson.

The brother whipped my legs with his cane so hard, it felt like I was getting an electric shock. We let go of the prefect and the brother dragged me by the hair at the side of my head out of the dining hall. By this time, reinforcements had arrived in the form of several other Christian Brothers, and order was quickly restored.

"He started it!" I shouted to the brother, as the tears of temper ran down my cheeks.

My explanation was ignored. I remember seeing boys scattering out of the way in fear of this brother as he dragged me down the corridor to his room. (I was later told by Paddy Rice that everyone was terrified of this particular brother, as he was very fond of dishing out severe beatings with his cane. I was soon to find this out for myself).

"Why did you start the fight in the dining room?" he snapped at me when we reached his office.

I tried to explain what had happened, although he had already made up his mind and my explanation was simply ignored. The office door burst open again and poor Alec was dragged in screaming by another brother. We knew we were in trouble and awaited our punishment. It was going to hurt, but nothing could hurt me as much as I had been hurt already, I thought to myself. I begged them to listen to me and said that Alec had nothing to do with the fight, but they were having none of it. The brother yelled at us both, saying that such behaviour would not be tolerated at St Peter's and that he was going to teach us a lesson. He obviously considered me to be a troublemaker.

The brother decided that I was to receive six strokes of the cane and Alec three for his involvement in the fight. Little did I know, but I was soon to experience physical pain like I had never done before. I was up first. The natural reaction of pulling your hand away as the cane is travelling towards it was not the best technique, as it simply earned me a slap around the head and another chance for the brother to swipe me with the cane. I was crying with the pain and my hand looked red raw. I remember the brother looking twice at Alec's hand when it was his turn and he quickly opted to whip his good hand. It may well have been the first time the brother had noticed Alec's missing fingers.

I really felt for my little brother, as he did not start the fight and was only trying to help me out, yet he also felt the wrath of the cruel brothers. It was never my intention to get Alec into trouble. After our punishment was over, we were taken back to our dormitory and we were told not to leave the room. Recreation time was missed and sore hands, as well as a few bumps and bruises were our badges of honour for the next day or two.

I wish the prefect who had picked on us had just left it there, but this was not the case and more run-ins with this bully were imminent. I was determined that I would not give in to him as I knew that if I did, he would make our lives even more of a misery than they were already at St Peter's. The idiot would do many things to try to get me in trouble, including knocking the bucket of water I used to cleaning the stairs with as he walked past. The bucket would spill down all the stairs and I would have to then clean up the mess quickly before I got in trouble with the brothers. He used to say nasty things to Alec also like calling him a freak. The bully-boy would always be with his little gang and never on his own when he did so. I swore to Alec that I would sort him out properly one day if I ever got a chance. I hated him.

Alec and I were allocated new seats in the dining hall on a different table than that headed up by the bully-boy prefect. We made friends with most of the other boys and we never really had much bother with anyone in the school from there on in apart, from with the idiot who had to try to throw his weight around with everyone. I think the other kids got the message that Alec and I did not look for trouble, but also that we would not run away from anyone, either. They soon learned that if they picked on one of the Porter boys, then they would have two of them to deal with.

Things quieted down after a while, as we tried our best to conform and get along in what was to be our home from there on in. One day whilst we were messing with the punch balls that hung in the corner of the gymnasium, Brother James, who was in charge of the sports equipment asked if we would like to join the school boxing team. With hindsight, I am sure he thought that doing so would help with some of the aggression that we both displayed when picked on by others. We agreed to join the team, even if it was to help stay clear of that prefect who seemed intent on getting us in to trouble.

We may have settled into living at St Peter's School, but we were never happy there. Alec and I would often get the blame if any scuffles broke out as a result of the other boys picking on one of us, and getting the cane became almost a regular occurrence. My job in the school was cleaning the floors of our dormitory and the stairs that led up to it. I had to wash and polish the area every week under the watchful eye of one of the brothers.

Alec and I joined the school boxing team and looked forward to training every Tuesday evening after tea. The gymnasium was great. There were climbing ropes, a vaulting box, a punch bag and a large mirror on the wall. Sometimes we would all go running around the football field outside and I would relish the feeling of being outdoors in the fresh air. Brother James was kind to us, and he would often make us laugh by telling us the tales of him growing up in Ireland. He was good to us and we liked him.

A few weeks after joining the school boxing club, Brother James told us that he had managed to get permission from the abbott to take us to train at a proper boxing club in the nearby town of Bury. We were going to get trained by a proper trainer, but what more importantly, we were going to be going outside of the school for the first time since we were taken there. It was a Wednesday evening, and once we had finished our food, Brother James took us to the boxing club in Bury where we met the trainer, a Mr Jelly.

We started to laugh when he told us his name but he said jokingly, "My name may be Jelly, but I am not soft."

He was a pleasant chap and he made us laugh and feel welcome at his boxing club. When he learned that Alec and I had come from Liverpool, he instantly warmed to us and said that he had trained some good boxers from the city. We felt at home with Mr Jelly. Going to the boxing club in Bury with Brother James every Wednesday was the highlight of our week. Both Alec and I now had even more of a reason to try to stay out of trouble at St Peter's School. We tried our best to behave and to do as we were told, as we knew that there was a good chance that they would stop us going to train at the boxing club in Bury if we did not. I just wished that idiot of a prefect would stay away from us.

We had some good news one Wednesday evening whilst we were training at Mr Jelly's gym. There was going to be a boxing tournament, with the fighters of his club fighting those of another club. He asked who was up for it, and Alec and I immediately volunteered. The tournament was on the following week. Alec was up first and he successfully defeated his opponent on points over three rounds of boxing. I was next up. My opponent stood in the corner of the ring before the fight and danced around in his flashy boxing shorts and a black and white vest. I was in the St Peter's standard issue gym shorts and my blue and grey vest.

The bell went and the bout started with this flashy little sod giving me a boxing lesson for the whole of the first round. My cornerman told me off at the end of the round. He said that I didn't move around the ring enough, and that I was making it easy for this kid to hit me and look good. The bell went for the second round and I charged out at my opponent like a mad man, swinging punches from all angles and generally trying to beat him up. The referee warned me for holding and when the bell went for the end of the second round, the red mist once again descended and I carried on pummelling my opponent until I was dragged off him by the trainers and referee. I got disqualified, and that was my first and last bout.

Mr Jelly was not happy with me and made me go into my opponent's changing room to apologise for my behaviour. This I did, and I was allowed to continue to train, but was not allowed to fight again for the club.

On the journey home, Brother James expressed his dis-appointment in my actions in the ring. He said that I had let the entire school down by losing my temper. To his credit, he promised not to say anything to the other brothers about my behaviour in return for me promising not to behave in that manner again. I appreciated this gesture of kindness from Brother James, as it surely saved me from more lashes with the dreaded cane.

Life at the school had become bearable, and although I would have liked to have learned more whilst I was there, the teaching methods of some of the Christian Brothers left a lot to be desired. They seemed to be more interested in punishment than in educating us. I remember one day sitting in my usual seat at the back of the class when the teacher began to hand out paper for a maths test. This test was different to the other tests we had previously had. We were told to put our names and numbers on the top of the page of the test sheet and then to start doing the sums in silence. I was competent at adding and subtraction, but I struggled when it came to sums involving multiplication and division. I had always copied the answers from the lad who sat next to me in the past and had never been caught out, so that is what I did on this occasion. The papers were handed back to the brother (I nearly said teacher, but that would not be a fair description of his role) at the end of the lesson.

The next maths lesson ended in the same way, whereby I handed my papers in to the brother as he walked past my desk in the direction of the front of the class. He eagerly scanned my work as he walked back to his desk and went on to shout loudly, "Porter. Come here!"

I could tell by the tone of his voice that I had been rumbled for copying the work from the lad who sat next to me. I made my way sheepishly to the front of the classroom and the brother in charge scribbled a long division sum on the board and the answer I had put on my test sheet and he asked me to explain to the class how I came about getting my answer. I froze on the spot as panic set in.

How could I possibly explain how I came out with the answer when I didn't have a clue on how to do the sum first? He knew this and was really enjoying making me look stupid. All the kids in the class were making fun of me and calling me names. The brother eventually told them to be quiet. He gave me the wooden board duster and told me to clean the board.

Instead of cleaning the board with the duster, I launched it at one of the lads who had been poking fun at me.

I achieved a direct hit, as the board duster clonked one of the main offenders right on the end of his nose, much to my delight.

Before my feet could touch the ground, I was whisked off to an office, where I was yet again told that my actions would not be tolerated. I was accused of refusing to do my maths paper and of throwing the board duster at another pupil. I was guilty of throwing the duster, but I simply could not answer the questions on the maths paper. As always, however, my explanation was ignored, and I was again given the cane. I was sent back to the dormitory, where I was made to scrub the bathroom floors for the rest of the day and evening. I wasn't bothered, as I knew someone would have told Alec what had happened to me, and at least he would have known where I was during the evening recreational period.

The next time I had a maths lesson, I just knew that I was going to be in some bother again, but I had no choice but to go to the lesson, so go to the lesson I did. This time, I had been moved to a desk in the front row, situated directly opposite the teacher. The so-called lesson began and the teacher again handed out test papers to everyone. I looked at the test paper questions and knew that they were beyond my capability and I simply could not work out the answers. As a result, I just put my name and number on the papers and sat there with the papers placed on my desk until the end of the lesson. When he picked up my papers at the end of the lesson and asked loudly so everyone could hear, "Porter. Why haven't you completed any of the questions on this sheet?" I replied, "Because I have never been taught how to do these sums, Sir."

The teacher implied that I was refusing to take the maths test and typically ignored my explanation. The bell rang and a brother came in and told me that I was to go with him to see the abbott. When we arrived at the abbott's office, he asked me why I was disobeying the teacher in class. Luckily for me, the abbott did give me a chance to put my side of the story, and I told him that I had struggled with the questions and could not complete the sums as I had never been shown how to. The abbott warned me that if I was lying then he would expose my dishonesty and that I would be severely punished for it. He then suggested that they sent for Alec's and my education record from St James School in Bootle to find out the truth. This time, he was to believe me.

The abbott told me to return to class and to obey the teacher always. He said that he did not ever want to see me in his office again. That suited me fine, as I never want to go there in the first place! The brother took me back to class and slapped me around the head whilst telling me I was a liar all the way. When I tried to speak, he simply growled at me to shut my mouth, as he did not believe a word that I said. The maths class was now over so he took me to the recreation hall, which meant even more slaps around the head from the brother as we walked. By this time, I was crying with temper and I immediately found Alec in the recreational hall.

"What have you done?" asked Alec. He could clearly see that something had happened, as I was upset and angry again.

"Nothing yet, Alec," I replied in temper.

That was the final straw for me, and I knew that we just had to try to get away from this place. We were going to escape and run away again.

"Alec, we are going to try to get away again," I whispered.

"Tommy, where can we go? Granny Porter doesn't want us, and the last time we went there, she called the police on us and they brought us back," Alec replied under his breath.

"Mickey, Johnny, Stevie, Edie and Mary must still be in Liverpool somewhere, so we will have to find them," I concluded.

Chapter Twelve

The Great Escape

The decision was made. We were going to try to escape and go home to Liverpool again. After a few days of me plotting our next escape, I decided that the best time for Alec and I to make a break would be on a Saturday afternoon, when we were all allowed to run around the football pitch as part of our training for the school boxing team. Brother James would keep an eye on us all, but this was surely our best chance to nip off and escape from this hellhole of a place.

The following Saturday, the big day, came around quickly for Alec and I. After lunch, we made a point of telling the other boys in the dormitory that we were going to watch a football match on the playing fields and then go for a training run around the field and grounds afterwards. Alec and I packed our kit bags with our training clothes and we left the dormitory for what we hoped would be the last time ever.

Once outside and near the playing fields, we wandered over towards the far end and took a chance to gain our freedom. We both scaled the high wall using the ivy that was growing happily on it. Before we knew it, we were over the wall and running as fast as our little legs would carry us, across fields and away from St Peter's School. I decided that we needed to get out of the fields as quickly as possible to avoid being spotted in the open and somewhat flat terrain, so we darted towards the railway track. This was to be our preferred escape route, as the angry search party would surely start by checking the busy roads nearby first. We ran and ran, fuelled by adrenalin and we were afraid to look back in case we were being chased. After a long time of running, the evening drew in and the darkness descended upon us.

Luckily we came to a railway siding before it got too dark. We knew what it was as we had seen many of them when we used to play on the railways in Bootle and there were lots of empty carriages there on several different tracks. We chose one and clambered up into the empty carriage and huddled together in the corner of the carriage to keep warm whilst we tried to get some sleep. Our home for the night was cold and uncomfortable, but we were together.

The next morning, we were woken up by a sudden jolting movement of the carriage. I quickly realised that the train was moving and when I looked out of the window, I could see that the train was being shunted into a station. We both jumped up and locked ourselves in the toilet of the carriage and waited in silence, as we could hear voices. Once it appeared quiet, I poked my head out of the toilet door and saw two men armed with mops and buckets making their way through all the carriages on cleaning duties. We got straight out of our carriage and hid underneath the bodywork of the train for a while.

I knew we could not stay hiding under the train for long, as it would surely start its journey soon. With this in mind, Alec and I crept underneath the train until we came to the very last carriage at the back. We then crawled up between the train and the platform and entered the carriage as covertly as our tired bodies would permit. The best hiding place for us seemed to be the little space under the seats that was usually reserved for small luggage, so we crawled into this space and did not say a word.

After a while, the train started to move. I remember hearing the doors banging as they were closed and the loud whistle of the conductor. Nobody got onto our carriage so I whispered to Alec that we would get off at the next stop and if we got caught, then we would say that we had lost our tickets. The train seemed to chug along the railway track for ages before we heard the noise of the brakes hissing away as they drew the machine to a halt at the next station. Before we had time to crawl out from underneath the seat and get off the train, two women got on the train and came into our carriage and slammed the door shut behind them.

"Shit," I thought to myself. We may have to stay hiding on the train for ages until these two women got off. Alec and I squeezed further under the seat, as far back as was physically possible, in an attempt to avoid capture. Alec soon started to wriggle a bit and I put my finger to my lips and gestured for him to remain quiet. His eyes filled up with tears as the train continued down the tracks. It became too much for Alec, and he started to sob.

The women bent down and screamed as they discovered the two stowaways under her seat. Once they had got over the shock of seeing us under the seats, they helped us out from the confined space and we saw that Alec had a large burn mark on the back of his leg where the hot water pipe of the train's heating system had burnt him quite severely. It was no wonder he had started to cry. One of the women pulled the emergency cord and the train stopped and the guard arrived at our carriage before we had chance to get on our toes again. The women told the guard that we had been hiding under the seats of the train and he asked us to produce our tickets. We stuck to our plan and told the guard that we had lost our tickets. However, we were stumped when he asked us which station we had got on the train at. The guard took us to the guard's van and told us that he would hand us over to the police at the next stop.

We explained to the guard that we were simply trying to get home to our family in Liverpool and although he said he felt sorry for us, he added that handing us over to the police was for our own good. At least he gave us some of his sandwiches and a cup of tea, as he could see that we were both hungry and we must have looked a sorry old state. As the train pulled up at the next station, I saw a large sigh saying Crewe. At the time, I did not know where Crewe was. We were taken off the train and into the station master's office, where we were met by two police officers.

"What are your names and where are you going?" the police officers asked.

"My name is Tommy Porter and this is my brother Alec. We are going back to our family in Liverpool, Sir."

"Liverpool?" the one police officer laughed. "If you're going to Liverpool, then why are you on a train that's heading south for London?"

This was never in the plan. We were on a train going totally the wrong way and we could have ended up on the streets of London if we had not been rumbled by those women. That may have been a better outcome than the one that awaited us on our return to St Peter's School.

The police officer then took my jacket off me and noticed the name of the school and my ID number that had been stitched into the garment. He quickly tore Alec's jacket off him to discover the very same school name, and we knew that we were not going to make it home on this occasion. The attitude of the police officers towards us changed instantly when they discovered the badge of St Peter's School stitched in to our jackets.

"How did you get on this train?" asked the police officer.

"We have run away, Sir, as the brothers are always hitting us and being cruel to us," I replied, hoping to get his sympathy and help.

"Well you must be naughty boys and deserve everything you get. We need to get you back to St Peter's straight away," he concluded.

To be fair to them, the police officers took us to the kitchen of the police station and they kindly gave us beans on toast. We were hungry and appreciated this gesture. The police officer gave us a stern telling off for walking on the railway and we were told tales of children dying as a result of being hit by trains whilst playing on the railway.

"It's okay, Sir, we always used to play on the railway when we lived in Bootle and no harm ever came of us then," I pointed out.

"You are a silly boy. Two of the Christian Brothers are on their way to collect you and they will take you back to St Peter's School," the police officer said.

Later on that evening, two brothers did come to the police station in Crewe to collect Alec and I, one of whom was Brother James, who made sure we knew that he was disappointed in us both for running away.

"I trusted you both and you both have let me and the school down again," he said.

"I'm sorry, Brother James, I really am, but we just wanted to go home to our family in Liverpool," I replied.

"You have no family now. We at St Peter's are your family now, and the sooner you get used to that, the better. Anyway, you are in big trouble when we get back to St Peter's," he said.

That was a conversation killer in the car if I'd ever heard one. Alec and I knew that we would be punished for our escape effort. Little did we know to just what extent the punishment was to be taken to this time. It was late at night when we arrived back to St Peter's, and all the lights in the building were switched off, as they were every night. This time, we were taken into the building by way of the private entrance, an entrance that neither of us had used before. This was not a good sign, and I could see the look of fear on Alec's face as we were marched inside the building. I was also scared, very scared, as I knew that we were in for some serious punishment at the hands of these sadistic so-called Christian Brothers.

Alec and I were taken into a large room that had oak panelling on the walls and what seemed to be a huge billiard table with a wooden top on it. Armchairs were positioned around the room and several angry-looking brothers were sitting there, waiting for Alec and I to be led to them. Alec was taken into another room away from me, and our interrogation soon began.

"You told lies to Brother James and you ran away from school, Porter," shouted one of the brothers aggressively.

"You have brought the police to the school, and this school will simply not put up with this sort of behaviour. You are trouble, boy!" growled another, whilst I stood terrified and sobbing in fear of what was about to happen.

I tried to explain why we ran away, but again, my explanation fell upon deaf ears. At this point my frustration and fear got the better of me, and I shouted back at the brothers as I tried to run out of the room to get to Alec.

"Why are you always picking on me and my brother? You always blame us for starting trouble and it's not always our fault. Why is it me that always get caned?" I yelled.

With hindsight, that probably wasn't the best move that I could have made at that particular time, as this incensed the so-called Christian Brothers even more. I was always going to get punished, but this little outburst in the name of trying to get fair play was going to cost me dearly.

The angry gang of brothers grabbed me by the arms and pushed me to the billiards table as I continued to shout as loud as I could at this cruel bunch of bastards. They continued to pull me onto the billiards table. They removed my trousers and pants and firmly held an arm and a leg each as I was spreadeagled over the billiards table. As you can imagine, I felt terrified and very vulnerable and dreaded what was coming next.

"I will beat the devil out of you, Porter!" screamed one of the men as the cane began to angrily rain down on my bare flesh in what was seemed like a festival of pain.

I was screaming for them to stop, as I had never experienced this level of pain before; it was terrible. They beat me to the point where I felt like I was going to become unconscious.

"That's enough. The boy is bleeding. Stop now," one of the brothers shouted to the one with the cane after what seemed to be an eternity lying face down on this billiards table with my legs and arms forced open wide in a star formation.

The beating stopped but the pain continued as I was removed from the table, still screaming.

My badly beaten and bleeding body was then taken to the bathroom where one of the brothers washed my back and bottom and applied some sort of cream, which also stung like hell. I was almost numb with the pain. I was give clean underpants and trousers to replace my bloodstained ones, which were then taken away for washing. Alec, who had also received the cane also but to a lesser extent than I, was then brought to the bathroom and it broke his heart when he saw what they had done to me.

"What have you done to my brother?" Alec shouted at the brothers in the room.

"That's what happens if you run away. You will get the same punishment if you do it again. Now shut up," growled one of the brothers.

Alec and I were then taken back to the dormitory. I remember him having to help me to put my pyjamas on, as it was an extremely painful exercise. I seemed to hurt from every pore. Every movement was a painful one, and I could hardly walk as a result of the cruelty inflicted upon me by these people.

That night I did not sleep a wink and when Sunday came around, I was allowed to stay in my dormitory instead of struggling down the corridors to go to mass. Was this because they didn't want everyone in the school to see the state I was in? I couldn't sit down for days. I would be checked over by one of the brothers daily and he would apply what I assumed to be antiseptic cream to my back and bottom. I will never forget that particular act of cruelty that they subjected me to when I was just a mere boy, and as for beating the devil out of me, I now hated the brothers more than ever.

About a week later, Alec and I were told to strip our beds, collect our clothes and to accompany a brother to the abbott's office. As we walked down the corridor, the brother told us that we were being transferred to another school. I knew that we were being moved because my beating a week earlier at their hands had gone too far and that it was easier for them to move us on than to possibly have to explain their level of cruelty to someone from the social services.

We entered the abbott's office. He told us that we were being transferred to another school, St Charles Roman Catholic School, which was in Brentwood in Essex. No further words were spoken. The door to the abbott's office opened and we were taken out into the pitch black of the night to a waiting car occupied by two different brothers that we had never seen before. I was not sorry to be leaving St Peter's, as our time there had been a living hell, and I said to Alec as I put my arm around his shoulders, "Anywhere is going to be better than this place, mate."

The car pulled off with Alec and I huddled together in the back seat with these new Christian Brothers in the front of the car and off we went on another journey into the unknown. We were on the move again.

Chapter Thirteen

Essex, Here we Come

The journey was a long one – we travelled in the back of the car for hours. Daylight faded and darkness fell and Alec and I did not have a clue where we were going. No clues were given as to where and when our journey would end; no words were spoken to us whatsoever for the duration of the journey. We never bothered asking the brothers where they were taking us. We had learned not to ask any questions regarding the decisions these people made.

After stopping several times at church houses along the route from St Peter's School to St Charles School in Essex for snacks and to use the toilet, again we arrived late in the evening at a set of imposing metal gates that dwarfed the car we were in. It was dark and the sight of this huge, well-lit school building at the end of a long driveway behind the gates was daunting. This place was a lot bigger than St Peter's School and I secretly prayed that our time here would not be as bad as it had been there. I also held a glimmer of hope that we would be reunited with our brother Paddy, but only time would tell.

The brother in the passenger seat got out of the car and wrestled the large gates until they opened wide enough for us to pass through. From there, we were driven up the long driveway to the main building. The closer we were getting to the building, the more the butterflies in my stomach seemed to flutter, as I wondered what awaited us here at St Charles Roman Catholic School. I just hoped that these Christian Brothers displayed a little more Christianity than the previous lot, but I wasn't going to count on that. It was the usual drill, whereby the car pulled up in the courtyard and we were collected from the car and taken inside by a Christian Brother.

The brother sat us in a room and left us alone for what seemed to be ages. Alec and I whispered to each other, wondering what this place had in store for us. We both knew what to expect, really, and quickly came to terms with the reality that this place would not be any different to how it was at St Peter's School as we knew this place was run by Christian Brothers and we knew how they ran a school. Whilst we were sitting in this room waiting to be lectured on the rules and regulations of the school, Alec and I made a pact that we would not put up with any nonsense from any of the other kids, as we had done at our previous school. We were not going to be intimidated by any of them.

After a while, three brothers entered the room where Alec and I had been waiting for our welcome committee. They introduced themselves as the headmaster and two teachers, and without any delay, the headmaster laid down the law with regard to what was expected of us.

"If you obey all the rules and instructions given by my fellow brothers, then you could be happy here. If you don't, then you will be punished and you will not have a happy time here. We will not tolerate any bad behaviour here at St Charles School," said the headmaster in a voice that sounded like he meant business.

The headmaster then went on to inform us that we would be placed in separate school 'houses' when it came to our lessons. I would be in one class and Alec in another. At this point, I plucked up the courage to ask, "Can we please sleep in the same room, Sir? We have always been together."

"You will sleep in dormitories, boy, however, I am sure this can be arranged," replied the headmaster. "I must warn you now, though, that if you try to run away from here like you did at your last school, then you will be separated forever."

I was relieved, as whatever was going to happen to us here, at least we would be together during the night and I could try to sleep knowing that my little brother was okay and was with me. I suppose it was also easier for them to keep an eye on us both if we slept in the same dormitory.

"Thank you, Sir. I promise we won't try to run away again. I just want to be with my brother," I said in the politest tone I could muster.

The official handover was now complete and we never saw any of the brothers from St Peter's again, which suited me fine, as I hated them. I guess they were also glad to see the back of me, too.

We left the headmasters office and were accompanied in silence by one of the St Charles Brothers along the highly polished wooden block floors of the oak paneled, somewhat spooky corridors of our new home. We climbed a large oak staircase and passed several statues of all the saints nestled in the walls and paintings of Jesus Christ along the way. I remember, as I passed the paintings which were proudly hung on the walls, hoping that this time Our Saviour may make his brothers be a little kinder to us than in previous establishments.

The brother did not speak a word to us until we arrived at a large room adorned with wooden benches all neatly arranged into rows and two long wooden tables with two older boys standing behind them, awaiting instruction from the brother. This sight was all too familiar. It was obviously time to get kitted out, ready for our stay at St Charles Roman Catholic School.

At table one we were issued with one blanket, one pillowcase and two sheets each. Table two issued each of us with a vest, underpants, a shirt, a jumper, short trousers, socks and a pair of boots. We were told to try the clothes on and we had to then parade in front of the brother for him to approve everything fitted us correctly. These clothes looked like they were brand new, unlike the ones we had been issued in the last school, so perhaps things would be a little better here, I thought.

Once we had been kitted out in our new school uniforms and our appearance had been approved by the brother, we were asked by one of these older boys what our names were. He filled in some forms and Alec and I had to sign them. I signed my form but as Alec signed his, I could see that the boys had noticed his missing fingers and their faces displayed a look of surprise as they stared at his hand. Here we go again, I thought.

We then left the clothing room and followed the brother along what seemed like a maze of corridors, passing numerous dormitories full of boys staring at us as we made our way to the dormitory that we were to sleep in. The brother pointed out which beds had been allocated to us and I was relieved to learn that our beds were relatively close to each other, as the head brother had promised when we met with him in his office earlier that day. The brother then called one of the boys over and told him that we were new boys and that he was to show us the ropes. The usual questions followed about where we were from and why were we there. He looked at us strangely when we spoke – I don't think he had ever heard a Scouse (Liverpool) accent before. I tried my best to be friendly towards this lad, as I did not want him to get the wrong impression and start off on the wrong foot.

I asked if it was the same sort of set up as the last school whereby we'd have a prefect at the dining table and I explained that I'd had some problems with the prefect at the previous school. The lad confirmed that there was a prefect assigned to every dining table at every mealtime and this prefect was nominated by the brother in charge of the dining hall. He explained that the job of the prefect was to make sure everything ran smoothly on their table and that everyone sat at the table stuck to the rules. Here we go again, I thought. I am going to let this prefect know that we will not be messed with from the outset.

After we had made our beds up with our newly issued sheets, blanket and pillowcase, our guide took us to the recreation area. Again, this was much the same as the one that we had been used to. It was a large room with oak-panelled walls and wooden block flooring, and had very large sash windows thta allowed the daylight to flood in. The room, which was full of boys, some younger and some older than we were, was equipped with a table tennis table, dart board and other tables where boys sat playing games. It seemed like the whole room stopped and stared as Alec and I entered. We went straight in and stood by one of the windows, looking out and pretending not to notice any of the other occupants.

As expected, it did not take long for a swarm of boys to surround us, questioning us and generally sussing us out. To my surprise, all the boys appeared friendly towards Alec and I, so this put me more at ease than I felt when we entered the room. This was a refreshing change from the last place, as there was always someone trying to come across as being the hard case there. There were the usual strange looks when they noticed Alec's missing fingers, so I decided to get it out of the way and tell everyone in a loud voice what had happened to Alec when he had his accident involving the lorry that sad day. "Wow! It's lucky he wasn't killed," one of the lads said in a Cockney accent.

This response to my explanation broke the ice with the group, and we continued to chat with them. They asked which dormitory we were sleeping in. A few of them were in the same one and said that they would show us back there when the bell rang. So far, so good. The bell rang to indicate the end of recreation time, and we accompanied our newfound friends along the corridors and up the wide staircase to our dormitory.

"Porter."

The brother who was in charge of the dormitories on our corridor shouted to me as we arrived at the door of our room.

"Have you got all of your bed clothes and have you been told the rules regarding the routine in the dormitory?"

"Yes, Sir. Thank you, Sir," I replied.

"If you have any questions, then ask me. If I am not available, then ask the prefect. I will not tolerate any bad behaviour in my dormitory. Is that clear?" he snarled.

We nodded our heads in confirmation and we continued to our allocated beds. In the time before lights out was called, I went, as I always did, and sat with Alec, as I knew how nervous he would be about his new surroundings. I reassured him that the other boys here seemed all right, but I knew that we would soon find out what they were really like over the next few days.

As before, I did not get much sleep at all on the first night in the new school. I pondered on how I was going to deal with the prefect at the dining table to ensure he did not treat us like the last one did. Most of the beatings by cane that I had taken from the brothers at our last school were because of that bullying and antagonising prefect. I was determined that this new prefect would not try to bully us. My backside and back was still red raw and bore the marks from the last beating I had received at the hands of the cruel brothers for running away from their school. These badges of pain and cruelty lasted well over a month on my body. I had a plan in my head.

The bell rang out loudly and weary faces emerged from their beds. It was morning and time to get up and ready for the day ahead. The first thing I did, as I did every day, was to look over to my brother Alec to make sure he was okay. Alec raised his hand to acknowledge to me that he was awake and that we had survived our first night at the new school. The first few days in all of these schools were incredibly stressful for Alec and I, as I am sure they were for all the boys who had been placed in the care of these places.

All the other boys in the room jumped out of bed and started stripping the blankets and sheets off their beds, so we quickly followed suit before the brother came in to inspect each bed. I knew that he would be looking to see who had wet the bed in the night and to make sure all linen was stripped from the beds in the correct manner. The brother entered and swaggered down the room whilst swishing his trusty cane in the air menacingly and banging it down hard onto each bed as he passed. He stopped at the bed of one unfortunate youngster who had obviously wet the bed (probably out of the anxiety and stress that was caused by living in such a regime). I felt for this lad, as I knew that would be punished somehow for this, although then I did not know just how it would be done. "Right. You know the drill, boy," screamed the Brother as he slammed his cane on to the iron bed frame in a temper.

The lad, who himself was soaked through to the skin with urine and was sobbing his heart out, was made to strip his bed and to roll up his mattress and tie it up with his bed sheet as we all looked on. He was then made to stand there by his bed, soaked and crying, until the brother had finished the room inspection. The brother in charge then sent us all, apart from the poor lad who had wet himself in the night, to the bathroom to get washed. Once in the bathroom, I enquired about the fate of this poor lad who had wet the bed. The rules were that if anyone urinated in their bed, then they would have to roll and tie up their mattress and then carry the mattress (which would be heavier than usual because it was wet) on his head down to the laundry room.

His walk of shame would see him having to parade his yellow-stained mattress as he walked past all the other lads from the other dormitories, who would be lining up in the corridors awaiting their turn to go in for breakfast. He would then have to wash the sheets by hand in the laundry room and wash down the mattress as best he could, before placing them in the drying room by the huge boilers that powered the hot water for the school. After doing this, he would then have to return to his dormitory to get washed and get himself ready to go down for breakfast. Later the same day, any bed wetter would have to return to the drying room to collect their mattress and sheets and again carry them back on their heads to the relevant dormitory. How humiliating was that?

The breakfast bell rang and Alec and I followed the others to the dining hall, where the brother on the door told us that we were to sit at table four. On the same table were a couple of lads that I had spoken to previously and they had been okay towards us. They were sitting next to a lad who was obviously the prefect for the table. I went straight up to this lad and said, "Are you the prefect on this table?"

"Yes, I am," he replied, standing up. "My name is Chris Johnson."

"Well, I am Tommy Porter and this is my brother Alec. We are new here and we are not looking for any trouble, but we won't be backing down from anyone, either," I said, as I eagerly awaited his reply. Much to my surprise and relief, the prefect replied, "There'll be no trouble. You just have to listen to the instructions given by the brothers or myself if you're sat in this table. It's my job to make sure everything is okay with my table."

I sat down feeling much better about it all now, as this prefect seemed to be pleasant enough and at least I had stood my ground and made my feelings clear to all those who listened in the dining hall that morning. From that day onwards, we never had any bother with Chris Johnson and got along with him just fine during our time at the school.

After we had finished breakfast, our new friend the prefect told Alec and I that we were to go back to the clothing room to collect our best clothes. These would be worn for visits to church on a Sunday and on other days of holy obligation, and of course, when the bishop or any other important visitors were on site. Our Sunday best clothes, as they were known, were dark blue in colour, and we had a blazer with the school badge stitched to the breast pocket. We were told that these clothes had to be neatly hung and stored in a locker in the dormitory that had our names on, and that they were only to be worn on special occasions, as previously mentioned. We had to clean our shoes every Saturday morning without fail.

The Sunday best clothes were allocated and we stored them according to our orders in the lockers before we went on to the classrooms for the first time since we had arrived at the school. I was to be in the yellow house and Alec in the blue house. One of the brothers then informed us of our jobs within the school, which would be undertaken at the weekends. I was to help out in the kitchen garden and Alec would help with school sports equipment. Most of my weekends would be taken up with digging, weeding and general gardening duties in the school kitchen garden, whilst Alec's job involved cleaning all of the football boots and ensuring that all the studs on them were in place and that the footballs were cleaned and had dubbing on them.

Alec also had to put all the dirty sports kits into the laundry basket ready for collection. He appeared to enjoy his weekend job at the school. At least if we kept busy, it took our minds off trying to get home to Bootle to find our family sometimes. We received payment of one shilling and six pence a week for our jobs, and the amount was recorded in our personal books. We could spend it in the canteen shop to buy sweets, colouring books, pencils or toothpaste (which came in a tin in those days), or just let it accumulate.

Lessons at St Charles were much the same as they had been previously and I continued to dread maths, as I simply was not very good at that particular subject.

I remember going for the first maths lesson at St Charles and looking horrified when I saw that the teacher had given me a desk on my own right at the front of the class in front of him. Who would I copy off from here? I knew I was in trouble. I sat down and was immediately embarrassed – I just knew the teacher was going to make a show of me in front of the others once my lack of ability became known to him.

Sure enough, we were not long into the lesson when he wrote some sums on the board for us to try to copy and work out the answers on our sheets of paper. I did the ones that I could, but this didn't amount to very many, as I really had no clue how to do the other sums. My paper looked almost blank and when the teacher came to collect the papers, he hit the roof in a frenzy of verbal abuse.

"Porter. You are not trying. Why have you not done your sums, boy?" he snarled as the class laughed at me.

Having been ridiculed again in front of a class full of my peers, I lost my temper and shouted back at him, "I don't know how to do the sums – that's why I haven't done them."

My temper starting building and I went on to kick my desk over, which incensed the brother even more.

He launched himself at me, and gripping my arms tightly, he dragged me out of the door of the classroom and made me stand there in the corridor on my own facing the wall in silence until the lesson was over. As I stood there waiting for the lesson to end, a small group of boys walked past and started taunting me and calling me names. A fight broke out as I went for the ringleader of the group and we wrestled on the floor. The teacher came out and rang a bell to raise the alarm and two brothers appeared from nowhere and ran down the corridor waving their canes in the air. After receiving a few whips of the cane, I loosened my grip on the lad who had been taunting me for standing outside facing the wall, and we were separated by the brothers.

Each brother grabbed one of my arms and they continued to drag me down the corridor to the headmaster's office. I knew what was coming next. I was getting quite used to it now. I was reported for not doing my work, and I was subjected to yet another caning. Six of the best as they called it; more like six of the bloody worst, if you asked me. My maths lesson hell went on for weeks: I could not do the work, the teacher would take me to the headmaster and I would get caned. It got to the point where I would refuse to even sit down at the desk in the lesson, so off I would be taken to the headmaster for more caning. It took many weeks for them to realise that I was being genuine and that I could not do the work the teacher was setting for me. Once the penny had dropped and they accepted that I was genuinely struggling with the subject, then I would have to go and sit in the headmaster's office with him whilst the other boys went to the maths lesson.

During my time spent in the headmaster's office, as opposed to being in the maths class, the headmaster would constantly tell me how I was making my own life a misery by disrupting classes and fighting with the other boys. I wish I could have told him how much of a misery my life had really become when my mother and father died and we had all been separated. I think the headmaster took to me and maybe even felt sorry for me, as he gave me the duty of collecting and delivering papers to the classes while I should have been in maths class.

My maths teacher continued to hate me, though, and he always made me wait outside his classroom whenever I called to his class on official duty. That was fine with me, as the feelings were mutual.

If I dared to step out of line when the maths teacher was around, anywhere in the school, he would jump at the chance of reporting me directly to the headmaster, no matter how petty the offence may have been. Even today, I am rubbish at maths, and it's no surprise as to why that is.

Apart from the maths teacher and the subject itself, I enjoyed my other lessons. The time my mother had spent with us reading when we were little had paid off, as I was good at it – in fact, better than most of the other pupils in the class. I also enjoyed history and geography. I used to spend hours studying the classroom globe and was fascinated by all the countries that were considered a part of the British Empire at the time. My mind would often drift to some far-off land in a form of escapism from the reality of my surroundings. I would also enjoy listening to the brothers telling stories from the Bible. However, my woodworking skills were not the best.

Alec seemed to settle in better after some time and he excelled at sports. He really enjoyed playing football. One day we were in the gymnasium and one of the brothers came over and offered us the chance to join the school cross-country team. Alec, who was a very good distance runner, jumped at the chance, and I guess I accepted if only so we could be together. I did not see Alec during lesson time as a rule, as we were in different classes, so the cross-country team gave us a chance to be together on some afternoons in the week whilst we trained.

The first training session for the school cross-country team soon came about. As a team of around 20 lads gathered at the school gates, we were told that we were all to run to Pilgrim's Hatch and back. This was apparently about five miles. We were also told that we would be timed to monitor our progress. I ran as fast as I could, but I was in the slower group and I just knew that long distance running was not for me. Alec, to his credit, ran alongside me all the way, but I knew that I was holding him back from achieving a time he was capable of. We completed the course that day and the teacher appeared quite pleased with the team performance. He said that our times would improve after more training, although I was not that sure.

After a few weeks of running the course, my time did improve, but I remained in the last group to finish each time. Alec, by this point, had established himself as one of the quickest runners in the team, and he would always finish in the top three. I had become friendly with a lad called Chris Clark. Chris was a good lad and we would run the cross-country course together. His running ability matched mine, and one day he said that he had come up with a plan for us both achieve better times for the run. His master plan for quicker cross-country times involved us taking a short cut that would allow us to catch the leading group on the return leg without anyone knowing any different.

He said that if we ran as fast as we could and tried to keep up with Alec for as long as we could, we could then nip off across the field halfway up the hill and rejoin them on their way back down the lane. Chris had worked out that we could finish in the middle of the pack as opposed to at the back if we took this shortcut. I thought it was an excellent idea, and we were ready to give it a go on the next training run.

Off Chris and I went, trying to keep up with the fast runners on the next training run. We lagged slightly behind the pack, as we did not want them to see what we were up to and because they were running too quickly for us to keep up with for long, anyway. Chris and I seized our opportunity and jumped over a gate halfway up the hill and we cut across the woods to the side lane that the runners would be soon passing on their return leg. We took cover in the hedgerow and waited for the front-runners to pass us before we leapt out of the hedge and continued to run down the lane until we finished in the second group of runners. As Chris and I passed the finish line, the brother in charge of the team was timing us and I could see the look of surprise on his face.

"Well done, you two. That is a big improvement. Keep up the good work," the Brother said in praise. Chris and I were well pleased with ourselves. The next time we had a training session, we did the same again. Despite cheating, Chris and I remained too slow to enable us to get selected to race, but at least we were no longer finishing in the last group of runners, as we had done before. Our plan continued to work well for a couple of weeks, until one day we discovered a change in the format of the cross-country run.

One day we had all gathered at the school gates in preparation of the cross-country run, and Chris and I were ready to pull our little stunt and finish well. This day was not as straight forward as usual. A different brother had the stopwatch and was in charge of starting the run. Minutes before we were set to start running, I nudged Chris with my elbow to alert him to the sight of the brother who was in charge of physical training, who had turned up in his shorts and vest whilst riding a bicycle. The whistle went and we all started running with the brother riding his bicycle behind us. Clarky and I knew that we had to try to run as fast as we could to avoid possible detection, but we were simply unable to make it out of the slowest group of runners. We did our best and hoped for the best.

At the end of the run, each boy was given his time as usual when we returned to the gym. After a shower, we were all called back into the gymnasium as the brother was going to announce which of us had been selected to represent the school at the forthcoming County Sports Day. I was so proud when Alec's name was read out, and he had a beaming smile on his face. The brother then read out all the average times of all runners, apart from the times of Chris and myself. Before I had a chance to even look over at Chris, we were both called out to stand in the centre of the gymnasium in front of the other boys. A silence fell across the room.

"Tell me, boys, why is it that your times suddenly improved dramatically, but when I followed you on my bicycle today, you struggled to get the same time as the first time you ran the course?" said the brother in a voice loud enough for everyone to hear.

I was convinced we had gotten away with it, so I was totally dumbstruck and said nothing, as I knew that any sort of reply would make things worse for Chris and I.

"We took a shortcut. It was my idea and Tommy just agreed with it," Chris said to his credit. Laughter erupted from the boys in the gym, and I could not help but smirk, but the brother did not see the funny side of it whatsoever.
"We'll see whose laughing now shall we? You have tried to make a fool out of me and you have let the entire team down," the brother yelled before dismissing the rest of the runners.

Another trip to the headmaster's office took place and again I had very sore hands for days, having received the cane again. Once our punishment had been dished out, we were then sent to then dormitory for the rest of the day and neither Chris Clark or I was allowed to train with the cross-country team again.

Alec continued to train with the team and was chosen to represent the school in numerous competitions, including running for the school at county level. I was so proud of my little brother and it made me happy to see him enjoying his sport at the school. The only thing I ever won at the school sports day was the wheelbarrow race, with Alec being the wheel. Oh, I did come second in the sack race once, and was proud of that achievement.

Chapter Fourteen

Altar Boy

St Charles Roman Catholic School featured a beautiful church, which we all attended regularly. The priest in charge of the church was a good man called Father Carl. Unlike the vast majority of the Christian Brothers, Father Carl would always take the time to speak with each of the boys as they left mass. He would also attend football practice, where he would always encourage us all to try our best and to enjoy our sporting activities. I warmed to Father Carl, as his kindness made him stand out from the others who were less kind.

During our daily visits to the church, Father Carl would sit us all down on the old wooden pews and tell us stories from the Bible. These stories fascinated me. I was always asking questions and paid full attention to his apparent words of wisdom. My interest in the Bible stories was soon noted, and Father Carl asked me if I wanted to become an altar boy. Being an Altar Boy at St Charles involved helping the Father out in what he called The House Of God at the weekends.

My weekend job at the time was that of a helper in the kitchen garden, which involved me digging, weeding and other menial chores, so I was well up for a change, and surely being an altar boy would be better than working in the garden, especially as it was winter at the time. I tried to get Alec to join me, but he was far too busy playing football on a Saturday, which was the practice day for the altar boys, so he declined. I would not have wanted to become an altar boy if Father Carl was not in charge there, as he was kind to me and I respected him.

So I became an altar boy, and I think that Father Carl was impressed with my knowledge of the Latin responses that we had to say during mass. I had become familiar with the responses and their related timings during the service when we used to go to St James Church on Marsh Lane in Bootle, before we were taken away from our family and into care. I was one of three boys who had agreed to undertake the job, and we agreed to attend lessons on Saturdays in order for us to learn how to carry out the duties during mass and on other occasions to the required standard. This was serious business.

The first Saturday came around and I went to the church where our training was to be held. I was issued with a frilly white shirt and a black cassock. I remember feeling really special being dressed up in all the gear. Once we were kitted out, Father Carl sat us down and reiterated that we had agreed to undertake a very responsible and special job, and that he would not tolerate any messing about in the House Of God and would be watching us very carefully during our training. We knew that any messing about would lead to us losing the job of altar boy and most likely, some form of punishment. I took the job seriously, and would get a little lump in my throat every time Father Carl told us that our parents would have been proud of us serving at the altar.

In those days, the whole mass was conducted in Latin, and Father Carl was very strict when it came to not allowing any talking, except for answering him when prompted. One of our duties was to help Father Carl to dress in his special robes. His wardrobe consisted of several different outfits that he would wear whilst conducting mass depending upon the time of the year. Other duties in the House Of God included us polishing the somewhat ornate candle sticks, the cross of Christ, the silver platter on which Holy Communion would be served and the silver challis. These items would have to be polished until you could see your face in them and of course, all this work had to be conducted in silence. I soon got the message that this was serious business and I enjoyed the trust and respect that Father Carl had put in us.

The House Of God, as Father Carl called it, featured a very long, solid wood table that looked old and impressive. The chairs that accompanied the table looked as if they had been carved for royalty to sit upon. At the end of the room, the altar boys had the use of a wooden locker that housed our lovely frilly shirts, cassocks and our smart shiny shoes, which we would only wear for altar boy duties. The priest had a row of large wooden wardrobe-like lockers in the room and these would house the most fancy of robes in beautiful colours that he would adorn for mass. All of his garments looked as if they had been stitched together with gold thread. I asked Father Carl where his robes came from, and he told me that they were made by the hands of the Holy Sisters in Ireland and that they must be handled with great care every time they were taken out of his lockers.

Mass at the church of St Charles School involved three altar boys, one positioned at the front of the priest and one each side of him. I always opted to sit on the left hand side of the priest, as this was the side that faced the general public who attended the service, while the Christian Brothers and boys from the school sat on the right. There were always some of the boys from the school trying to catch my eye during mass and put me off my duties so I would get into trouble, so being on the side that did not directly face them made my job a little easier.

Altar boys had to concentrate during the service, as we were expected to remember every move that the priest would make. We had to ensure we were in the right position at the right time, and it all had to look like a smoothly-run operation in front of the congregation. We soon learned that Father Carl would not be best pleased if he had to look to see where we were during the service, so we all learned our roles and the associated positioning quickly. We practised until it became second nature to us. We all took the roles seriously and enjoyed our little bit of responsibility. We tried hard to please Father Carl.

As altar boys, we usually served with Father Carl, but as we slowly became better at it, we started to serve with other priests from the parish occasionally. I remember one priest called Father John who made me smile when we were preparing for Holy Communion during mass.

At a certain point in the service, the altar boys would approach the altar in preparation of filling the challis up with red wine and water to symbolise the blood of Christ during the communion.

Father John would always lift the arm of the altar boy who was pouring the red wine so that he would fill the challis to the maximum. I would then go to pour the water into the challis as we had been trained to do, but Father John would put his hand over the top of the challis after I had poured a small drop of water in the vessel. He would then neck the entire contents of the challis in one gulp, much to our amusement. The altar boys never dared to say anything to anyone about his fondness for the holy wine, but we used to have a little chuckle about it between ourselves after mass.

It was the job of one of the altar boys to carry the incense burner up to the top of the altar during mass, and then kneel in front of the priest. Whilst carrying the burner, you would have to swing it from side to side to keep the flame alight on its journey. Another altar boy would then carry the incense granules in a highly polished silver bowl with a silver spoon, and he would also kneel in front of the priest. On one particular day, the church was full as it always was, and I was charged with the task of carrying the incense burner to the altar. I walked up to the altar, enthusiastically swinging the incense burner as I'd been trained to do, before it was filled with granules, the top was closed and it was passed over to the priest.

Father Carl began swinging the incense burner as he walked around, but this time the church quickly filled with smoke and it soon became apparent that the granules had been tampered with. The congregation coughed as everyone inhaled smoke. Father Carl had a face like thunder. He gave me the incense burner and instructed me to remove it from the church immediately. I took the incense burner and emptied it into the garden at the back of the church. A post-mass investigation soon began. The suspicious contents were gathered from the garden and Father Carl discovered bits of candle wax mixed in with the granules of incense.

The fingers of suspicion soon pointed at me, but when Father Carl checked the tin that contained this batch of granules, he found more candle wax, so I was given the benefit of the doubt on this occasion, and rightly so.

I served as an altar boy with Father Carl for the rest of my stay at St Charles Roman Catholic School, and I always looked up to him, as he was a kind person who treated us well.

Apart from a few initial skirmishes with some of the other boys in the school, Alec and I settled in well to St Charles School. From the outset, we were determined that we would not be bullied by anyone, and we often got the blame for starting the fights, although it was not always the case. Overall, the majority of the boys in the school knew we would fight back if they tried to bully us, so they left us alone and we got on with our lives as best we could during our time there.

Chapter Fifteen

Christmas Cheer

As a child, I can honestly say that I cannot recall ever having a birthday. Each day was much the same as another; we would get up and go and play with the other kids on the street. Christmas was a little special, though. On Christmas Eve, before going to bed, we used to hang up a sock on the mantelpiece in the house and if we were lucky, we would wake up on Christmas morning to find in the sock an apple, orange and some nuts packed out with cinders from the fire. Times were hard, there were 12 children in the house and often no work for our dad. Everyone in our area at the time seemed to be in the same situation, and we thought nothing more of it, as that was the norm to us.

At St Charles Roman Catholic School, Christmastime was a little different as Alec and I soon found out. It was tradition at the school that some of the boys would be fostered out temporarily with Catholic families that attended the church. I remember standing in the line with all the other pupils of the school whilst the names of the lucky pupils were being read out. These pupils would be spending Christmas with families, as opposed to staying in the school, like those whose names were not on the list.

Alec and I had not been chosen to be fostered over the Christmas period, and we were to remain with the 20 or so other boys who also had to stay in the school with the brothers. We didn't mind too much, as at least we would still be together. I later found out from one of the boys that it was the Christian Brothers at the school who got to choose which pupils would spend Christmas with the families. He told me that any pupil that had wet the bed or had been involved in any form of bad behaviour would not be considered, so that was Alec and I out of the picture. We had never wet the bed, but had found ourselves on the wrong side of the rules a couple of times. A couple of days before Christmas, those of us who were staying behind were taken out into the yard to wave off the boys dressed in their best clothes that were usually reserved for Sundays and other important religious occasions.

The next day was Christmas Eve and after we had finished breakfast, the headmaster summoned all of us to the courtyard at the front of the school. My mind instantly thought of what I may have done to merit another telling off, but I was to be pleasantly surprised. Twenty or so of us stood in the courtyard and our jaws dropped in amazement when we saw a jeep and two big army trucks coming towards us up the driveway of the school. We were all very excited. I noticed that they had big white stars on the front of the vehicles, so I knew that they were American soldiers. I had seen photographs of similar vehicles back in Bootle, so I hoped that there was not another war on.

The US Army vehicles came to a halt in front of us on the courtyard and the American soldiers swung down off the back of the trucks on ropes that were attached to the canvas framework. We all stood wondering what was going on, until the headmaster explained that the American soldiers were going to kindly take us out for the day. He went on to say that the soldiers had come from their Army base in Essex as, like us, they were unable to spend Christmas with their families back home, so they wanted to spend a day with us. Wow! This promised to be the best day that we'd had for quite some time, and Alec and I could hardly contain our excitement.

Each soldier would take charge of a pupil when the commanding officer and headmaster walked along the line of pupils together, with the headmaster reading out our names. When he called my name, a big black sergeant came over and put his arm around me. I was a bit nervous, as I had previously only seen a black person in pictures or occasionally when we played on the Dock Road back in Bootle and we saw a merchant sailor who had travelled from afar – but he seemed very friendly and I soon felt at ease.

After all the boys had been introduced to the soldiers and a brother had got into the cab of each truck, us boys all boarded the huge green Army trucks and we sat excitedly in the back with our new soldier friends, not knowing what was going to happen next. This was great fun. Alec had boarded the same truck as I had and we both sat next to each other with massive smiles from ear to ear.

Each of us sat next to our US military buddies as the trucks left the school grounds and we travelled down to the nearby town, where all the people waved to us as we passed them by. The truck drivers were sounding their horns all the way, and every one of the boys on the trucks was absolutely delighted. Things soon got even better when one of the soldiers told us that they were taking us to the fairground for the day. We felt special and happy.

The day out at the fairground turned out to be fantastic, and was thoroughly enjoyed by everyone. The soldiers were ever so kind to us and they bought us candyfloss, ice cream and hot dogs. We must have gone on every ride in the fairground. This was one of the happiest days of my life that I remember to this very day, all these years later. On the way back from the fairground, the trucks stopped and we all got off and went into a cafe where we were treated to tea and cakes by the soldiers. We sang Christmas carols to the soldiers in the back of the truck on the way back to school as a way to say thank you to them for their kindness. They were all lovely people and I wished that the day would never end.

When we arrived back at the school and climbed down from the huge trucks, the soldiers went over to the jeep that had accompanied their trucks into the school grounds earlier that day. Each of the soldiers gave a Christmas present to the boy they had been looking after that day and they told us that we were not to open them until Christmas morning. The headmaster then thanked the soldiers for what they had done for "his boys", as he called us. I was surprised by this remark, as he didn't seem all that fond of any of us usually. The US Army Officer said that the day had been a real pleasure and that they were happy to try to make it a happy Christmas for us all, as they knew we had no family to do it.

The soldiers gave us all big hugs. Many of them had tears in their eyes as they said their goodbyes and climbed back into their vehicles before leaving the school grounds, sounding the horns of the trucks all the way. That day was the first and last time I ever saw an American soldier, and the memory of the kindness they showed to us all that day will stay with me forever. The soldiers left and we were told to put our name on the present that had been given to us. The brothers would then take the presents away for safekeeping for us until Christmas morning, after we had been to mass.

That night as I lay on my bed in the dormitory, exhausted after such an action-packed day courtesy of those very kind American soldiers, I thought about how happy both Alec and I had been that day. My mind soon drifted back to Marsh Lane. I thought of my family and whether they were as happy as Alec and I had been that day. I promised myself that one day, I would find them all, before I cried myself to sleep again.

We woke up on Christmas Day and adopted the usual routine of getting washed and dressed – only this time, it was into our best clothes, as we were to attend a special Christmas Day mass in the church. All the boys in the dormitory got ready and went down for breakfast. All of us apart from those who had wet the bed, I must add, as they were subjected to the usual punishment of carrying their wet mattresses and linen above their heads down to the laundry and drying rooms.

Everyone seemed excited about the thought of opening the presents that the soldiers had given us. Alec and I had never seen a present wrapped up like these, and we were dying to get our hands on them. Breakfast was rushed, and we enthusiastically went to mass in our best clothes, as we knew it would soon be present time. After mass, we all went to the recreation room and waited intently for the brothers to bring in our Christmas presents.

The brothers soon came into the recreation room and distributed the presents according the names written on them. Each of us quickly ripped open the wrapping paper to find out what treat was in store. Alec got a game and to my surprise, I got a box of chewing gum. Everyone was showing each other what they had received. One of the boys had received a toy pump action rifle that fired small table tennis balls and all of a sudden, his present looked far more appealing than my box of chewing gum. I asked him if he wanted to swap gifts and although he did not really seem that keen in the beginning, he seemed to warm to the idea after a while and some constant nagging. Anyway, we swapped gifts and he had the chewing gum and I had the toy rifle.

All was well until later that day, I found out that the lad who had swapped gifts with me had found a five-pound note in the bottom of the chewing gum box and he was bragging to everyone about his lucky find. As you can imagine, I was not happy and I wanted to re-exchange gifts as that five pounds was meant for me. I had never had five pounds before, so I went to find him and asked him nicely for the chewing gum and the money back, but he said no and clung on to the items like a vice when I tried to snatch them back.

Things soon escalated and a crowd of boys gathered around us both as we started fighting over ownership of the treasure. I hit the lad over the head with the toy rifle and it snapped in two, but little did I know that two of the Christian Brothers were making their way to the scene and they had seen me doing this.

"Porter is trying to steal my Christmas present, Sir," the boy told the brothers as they separated us both from the fracas.

Yet again I tried to explain myself and I said, "I was not trying to steal anything. It was my present in the beginning."

"We swapped gifts and when Porter found out that there was money in the present, then he wanted it back, Sir," the boy went said.

The brother immediately took the money off the boy, as having money was not permitted under any circumstances. He told him that it would be put into his personal savings for him to use as he wished another time. The brother then handed me back the broken toy gun and whisked me off to the headmaster's office. By this time I was crying in temper and not only had I been left with a broken gun, but chances were I was going to get the cane from the headmaster.

"Porter, can't you behave? Even on Christmas Day, you are causing trouble," the headmaster said in a very non-festive tone.

Again my explanation of what really happened fell upon deaf ears and I was given six lashes of the cane, before being confined to the dormitory for the rest of Christmas Day. So I did not get anything for Christmas that year except a sore backside. The so-called Christian Brothers at St Charles Roman Catholic School were still willing to dish out the cane even on Christmas Day. Merry Christmas, I thought to myself.

Chapter Sixteen

At the Seaside

Life at St Charles Roman Catholic School became better for us as time went on. Alec and I were getting a bit more peace from the older boys at the school compared with when we first arrived. They knew that I would fight back, no matter how many times I got beaten with the cane for doing so. Despite the majority of the boys at St Charles School getting the message, occasionally we would come across the odd boy or two who still tried to throw their weight around in an attempt to show that they were a hard case. They would try to pick on Alec or myself and make life uncomfortable for us.

When this happened, I would start by politely asking them to leave Alec and I alone, but more often than not, this would not work and things would escalate with them starting to push and shove before progressing to a fight. I did not care who I fought and sometimes I got a hiding from the older boys, who were much stronger than I was. Despite this, I would not give in to them and I would always get up and go back for more until they got the message. As far as I was concerned, I had lost my parents and family, apart from our Alec, and I had nothing left to lose, so getting the odd hiding and lashing with the cane did not really bother me.

Every time someone picked on me and I fought back, it was me that got taken to the headmaster's office to receive a verbal ear-bashing and a whack or six with the cane across my arse. The lads who I was friendly with in school were puzzled and did not understand why I could not just walk away at the first sign of bother and so avoid getting into trouble. They must have thought I was a little crazy, but as far as I was concerned, I was determined not to let these bullies pick on Alec and I to make our lives even more of a misery. We were suffering enough heartache and misery without these idiots contributing to it.

As time went by, the brother who was in charge of the dining hall appointed me as prefect for table five in the hall. This was clearly an attempt to help me settle and to perhaps give me a position that would help the others in the school accept me into school life at St Charles. I agreed to do the job on the condition that Alec could sit at my table. I promised myself that I would treat all of the pupils nicely and do my job to the best of my ability.

Each table consisted of ten boys and the rules of the dining hall were to be strictly adhered to always. As prefect, it was my responsibility to ensure that my table behaved and followed these rules to the letter of the law. I went out of my way to be nice to every boy that sat at our table and it seemed to pay off, as we had less bother in the school as a result. The brother in charge of the dining hall also left me alone and even began to speak to me nicely as time went on.

School life at St. Charles was competitive, as I am sure it was in most schools then. On Sports Day, each table would act as a team and would compete against the other teams. This was great fun and we got to take part in all kinds of races, such as the three-legged race, sack race, wheelbarrow race, hurdles, and running around the track. The finale was the cross-country race. Luckily for our team, Alec was a very good runner, so we always won a few of these races. We looked forward to Sports Days, as they brought a welcome dose of fun to the school.

One day, just as we had cleared our table after having dinner, the brother in charge told Alec and I to accompany him to the headmaster's office. I immediately felt sick, as we had not been in trouble or done anything wrong, so I thought that they were going to move us again. Here we go again, I thought, as I looked at Alec and smiled to reassure him that everything was well.

Upon arriving at the headmaster's office, we were pleasantly surprised when he told us that a couple who lived in the local parish wanted to take two pupils out of the school for the weekend and that Alec and I had been chosen. He told us that he would allow this to happen if we promised to behave. Initially, I suspected that he was telling us a pack of lies and that we were really going to be moved on again, or worse still, separated. A minute or so passed by with me standing there with a dazed look on my face whilst my mind raced, before the headmaster's words finally sunk in and I realised that he was genuine and that Alec and I really were going to get taken out for a weekend.

We were both so excited and hugged each other in delight as we had not spent much time (permitted time, anyway) out of the homes since we had been taken away from our family at Holywell Road in Bootle what seemed to be a very long time ago.

A week had passed since the headmaster had told us about our weekend out, when one of the brothers came to us on a Wednesday afternoon and told us to gather our Sunday best clothes from our lockers and to pack them into a suitcase that he gave us. We both packed our best clothes into the suitcase with smiles that spanned from ear to ear, before the brother checked the contents to make sure that we had everything we needed for our weekend out of the school. We carried the suitcase to the headmaster's office and he told us that we were to leave it there with him as Mr and Mrs Brown (I cannot remember their names, so I will call them Mr and Mrs Brown) would be coming to collect us from the school on Friday morning.

The headmaster reminded us that we were to be on best behaviour, although he really did not need to, as Alec and I were so happy to be getting out of the school, even if just for a weekend. We thanked the headmaster and returned to the dining hall. All the boys were asking why we had been taken out of the hall earlier and what was going on. Whilst walking back from the headmaster's office, Alec and I had agreed not to tell any of the boys anything about it, in case some tried to spoil it for us.

Friday morning soon arrived, and we were very excited and a little nervous, as we did not know what to expect. Alec and I were both very anxious about meeting these people. As Alec and I waited in a room next to the headmaster's office with one of the brothers, I asked him, "Why have Alec and I been chosen to go out for the weekend?"

"Because you have both settled down well at the school, Porter, and the headmaster hopes that your behaviour will continue to improve if you go out for the weekend," replied the brother.

We were then called into the headmaster's office and I was surprised to see Father Carl alongside the Headmaster and Mr and Mrs Brown. We were introduced to the Browns and the headmaster gave the couple a brief of who we were and where we had came from.

"Alexander and Thomas are very close, and they are happy as long as they are kept together. We have tried to keep them together since the death of their parents," he went on to say. At this point, Alec and I started to cry and I quickly wondered where our brothers and sisters may be and if we would ever see them again.

"I have always found both boys to be polite and trustworthy, and Thomas has served very well as an altar boy. I am sure that they will have a lovely weekend with you, Mr and Mrs Brown," Father Carl added. Father Carl then took Alec and I back into the room next to the headmaster's office as the Browns and the headmaster continued talking. Father Carl told us that Mr and Mrs Brown had no children of their own, so they would often take boys from the school out for weekends and holidays to help prepare them for life outside school when the time came. What kind people, I remember thinking to myself.

We were to leave after lunch on the Friday and we would be in the care of the Browns until lunchtime on the Monday. Just before we left, both Father Carl and the headmaster asked us to be on our best behaviour for the weekend. They reminded us that Mr and Mrs Brown were good people who had done much work for the school and the parish. I realised that this was a rare opportunity to spend some time away from the school and to mix with people other than the brothers and pupils of St Charles. I had no intention of letting Father Carl down, as I respected the man so much.

Alec and I almost skipped out of the school and into Mr and Mrs Brown's big car, in which they kindly drove us to their house in Brentwood, Essex. After some time in the car, we turned off the main road. Alec and I grinned in the back seat as the tyres of the car made a crunching sound on the gravel driveway and we approached a lovely big house with prominent bay windows at the front. "Wow", I said in amazement, as I had never seen such a beautiful house before.

The Browns, who seemed to be genuinely lovely people, made us feel very welcome and totally at ease in their home very quickly. Mrs Brown showed us to our bedroom, which had two single beds and a bathroom directly next door. There was even wallpaper. This was luxury, serious luxury! We were shown the wardrobes in which we could hang our clothes and then Mrs Brown left us alone in the bedroom.

"Come down and have dinner with us when you are ready," Mrs Brown said in her soft voice.

We enjoyed a hearty home-cooked meal with Mr and Mrs Brown, and I remember looking across the dining table to Alec with a massive smile on my face. This was the best meal we had had in a long time and it was almost strange, as we both were happy again. I just knew that we were in for a lovely weekend with these generous and kind people.

After dinner we sat with Mr and Mrs Brown in their lounge and talked about our childhood. They seemed very interested in our upbringing in Liverpool and the happy times we had spent with our brothers and sisters before our mother and father had died. They seemed fascinated when they found out that there were 12 children in the family and a little shocked when they found out how young our parents were when they died.

"It sounds like you had a happy home until your parents sadly passed away," Mr Brown said. Alec and I nodded, as I guess we just could not get our words out at that particular time. The Browns appeared surprised and sympathetic towards us when they learned that we had been moved so far away from the rest of our family; all the way to the South of England. They reassured us that we would one day be reunited with our brothers and sisters. I really hoped so.

Later that evening we wished Mr Brown goodnight and Mrs Brown took us to our bedroom, where we put on our pyjamas. She then tucked us both into our beds and told us to simply knock on their bedroom door if we needed anything during the night, before she wished us goodnight and left us alone. Alec and I lay there on comfortable mattresses with our heads on the soft pillows and we talked well into the night about how kind Mr and Mrs Brown had been to us. We wondered what the weekend would hold for us. For once, we both fell asleep feeling comfortable and happy.

The next morning, we awoke to the sound of someone knocking gently on the bedroom door. It was Mrs Brown. "Good morning, boys. Did you sleep well?" she asked.

"Yes, Mrs Brown. We both had a lovely sleep. Your beds are very comfortable. Thank you," I replied politely.

This was quite different from our usual wake-up call by one of the brothers shouting at the top of his lungs and making fun of those boys who had wet their beds. This was a different world; a world which I much preferred!

"Breakfast will be ready when you have washed and dressed, so we will see you in the dining room," Mrs Brown said.

Alec and I washed, dressed and made our way to the dining room of their lovely home and we both sat there quietly in appreciation of the breakfast that was to be provided for us. Mr Brown joined us at the dining table and Mrs Brown soon brought us a bowl of porridge each, followed by a plate full of bacon and eggs. We even had toast and a cup of tea. This was the best breakfast I had ever eaten, and we were both so grateful for their kindness.

"Have you ever been to the seaside, boys?" Mrs Brown asked after we had finished eating our hearty breakfast.

"Yes, Mrs Brown. We once went to New Brighton over the water on the Mersey ferry," I replied. Mrs Brown smiled.

"How would you like it if we went to Brighton on the south coast?" she asked.

"Yes, please, Mrs Brown. That would be lovely," I quickly replied, although I didn't have a clue where we were, never mind where Brighton was.

Just before lunch, we all got in their car and Mr Brown drove us to the seaside. I remember Mr Brown smoking a pipe all the way as he drove to Brighton. I will never forget the strange, sweet smell of his burning tobacco. I liked the smell. Throughout the journey in the car, Mrs Brown was telling us all about the seaside and Alec and I enjoyed every minute of the journey. We were very excited.

We stopped at a cafe on the way to Brighton, and Mr and Mrs Brown kindly bought us some lunch. It was here that they told us that they did not have any children of their own and that they had both retired from their jobs, so they were happy trying to make a little difference in the lives of children like Alec and I, who had no family to look after them, hence their involvement with St Charles School. Our journey then continued and we soon reached our destination by the sea, Brighton.

Mr Brown parked in the car park of a hotel on the seafront. The butterflies in my stomach woke up and Alec tugged my sleeve (as he did when he was nervous) as we all walked into the hotel reception area. Alec and I had never even been in to a hotel before, never mind stayed in one overnight. Mr Brown checked us all in at the reception desk and we were shown to our rooms. Alec and I had a room to ourselves, which was great. Mrs Brown accompanied us to our room and helped us unpack our clothes before we went downstairs with her to the dining room for dinner.

The food was wonderful, and there was plenty of it. Alec and I made the most of it and ate as much as we could. After dinner, we went with the Browns for a walk along the seafront promenade. The beach appeared to be full of pebbles and there was not as much sand as we had seen at the shore back home in Bootle. We walked and talked our way along the promenade until we came to the pier, at the entrance to which were two large statues of laughing police officers. Alec and I found these statues amusing, and we laughed and laughed at the sound that they made.

Our walk continued along the promenade, and we were treated to ice cream. We had never tasted ice cream before; it was lovely. We all sat in a shelter on the front watching a group of children playing happily in the water as we devoured our delicious ice creams. By this time, we were both tired, so Mrs Brown took us up to our room and put us to bed when we got back to the hotel. "Goodnight and God bless you," were the words with which Mrs Brown ended our lovely day.

The next morning, after breakfast, Mr and Mrs Brown took us back to the promenade and this time, we went onto the pier. We spent the entire morning at the fairground there, and we must have gone on every one of the rides. This was so much fun, and it was the happiest Alec and I had been for quite some time. We returned to the hotel at lunchtime for food before we set off on a drive in their car along the south coast, stopping off for some food at a cafe on the way, before returning to the hotel after an action-packed day. Alec and I went to bed that night a pair of very happy boys.

As the next day was Sunday, we accompanied the Browns to mass; after which we again spent the driving around on a sightseeing mission around the south coast of England. Both Alec and I loved seeing the different places and sights along the way as we happily chatted with the Browns, who once more treated us to lunch at a cafe en route. We returned to the hotel, had our evening meal and that evening, we had a long chat with Mr and Mrs Brown. They wanted to know more about Alec and I and how we had been treated by the different brothers in the homes.

I did not tell them about all the trouble I had been in or about the beatings and cruelty I had received from the brothers, as they were well-respected in the parish and I did not want to cause any trouble for the school. I knew that if I did, there would be repercussions and that I would be punished yet again. Again, that night, Alec and I went to bed very happy. We did not want this weekend to ever end.

Sure enough, Monday morning came about and we packed our suitcases and ate some breakfast in preparation for our journey back to Brentwood with Mr and Mrs Brown. We stopped at the home of the Browns for a cup of tea and a final chat before they took us back to the school, having thoroughly enjoyed their company. Mrs Brown hugged us both. This was the first hug and affection we had experienced for what seemed an eternity. For a split second, my mind was happily in the safety and comfort of the loving arms of my mother.

Upon our arrival at the school, we were met by a brother, who took us all straight to the headmaster's office. The headmaster asked me, "Have you had a good time this weekend with Mr and Mrs Brown, Thomas?"

"We have had a wonderful time sir. It was great. Thank you," I replied enthusiastically.

"We have all had a lovely weekend and both of the boys have been a joy to be with. They have both behaved impeccably and are such polite and well-mannered young men. We hope to do it again in the future," Mrs Brown told him as she smiled at Alec and I.

"Thank you very much, Mr and Mrs Brown." Alec and I said in harmony. "We have had a lovely time with you both and you have been very kind to my brother and I. We have not been this happy for a long time. Thank you very much," I went on to say.

We said farewell to Mr and Mrs Brown and Alec and I left the headmaster's office in tears and went back to the dormitory where we would resume the routine of life at St Charles School. The brother who walked with us back to our dormitory told us that we could very well see the Browns again one day if we continued to behave. I promised myself that I would try my best not to fall out of favour with the regime, but under such circumstances, I could only take each day at a time. I really wanted to spend more time with Mr and Mrs Brown.

I will never forget Mr and Mrs Brown and the kindness that they showed us, and I often wondered what life may have been like if they had fostered Alec and I. Some families in the parish of St Charles had fostered boys from the school, but I guess that it may have been a little too much to ask of the Browns to foster two lively lads like Alec and I at their time of life. We would have had to come as a pair, as there was no way we would be separated. I wish that later in life, I could have met up with Mr and Mrs Brown to thank them again for being so kind to us.

Chapter Seventeen

On the Move Again

Just as life in St. Charles Roman Catholic School was starting to become a little more bearable, we were in for another twist of fate. It was a lovely sunny day, and we had all just eaten breakfast in the dining hall when the headmaster made a grand entrance and demanded silence, asking every boy to sit at their table immediately. This was worrying, as throughout the duration of our time at this school, the headmaster had never done this. All were present at my table, but some boys from other tables were in the laundry room washing their bedding, having wet their beds during the night, so they were immediately rounded up and we all sat in silence as the headmaster made his announcement. I knew that his was going to be serious news.

"St Charles Roman Catholic School is to close at the end of the month. You will all be relocated to other Roman Catholic Schools, however, you will all not be going to the same school," the headmaster said in a loud and firm tone. I felt my heart thumping in my chest as my mind raced. Would this mean Alec and I would be split up? Alec was hanging onto my sleeve again, as he was also scared of what was to come. All the boys began whispering as we wondered where we would be taken next.

"Quiet! I have not finished," yelled the headmaster to quell the whispering in the hall. "St Charles Church will remain open, but the school is to close. Each of you will be told to which school you will be going once arrangements have been finalised in the next few weeks."

All the occupants of the dining hall were in shock. My head was now spinning and I wondered how Alec and I would live life without each other if we were taken to different schools. I felt physically sick. Alec was as pale as a sheet and was mentally tugging on my sleeve again. This was bad news.

That night, before lights out in the dormitory, Alec and I sat together disheartened and anxious as we discussed what may become of us due to the pending closure of the school. Alec and I agreed that I should try to talk to the Christian Brother who was in charge of the dormitory; to ask him where we may be sent and if there was a chance that we could stay together. It was not as simple as sitting down with the brother, as we first had to gain the permission of the prefect of the dormitory to speak to him. As lights-out time was approaching, I went to see the prefect of the dormitory to ask him for permission to speak to the brother the next day and he reluctantly said that he would ask him and he would let us know the next day. My brother and I went to bed and eventually drifted off to sleep in an anxious and sad state of mind again.

In what seemed no time at all, the rising sun shone through the windows of the dormitory to awake me from my restless night of slumber. It was almost as if I had not been to sleep. Our hopes were raised when the prefect told us, after we had made our beds, washed and dressed as we did daily in our military-like regime, that the brother in charge of the dormitory had agreed to talk to Alec and I at bedtime that evening. We were grateful, and I spent that day pondering how I would ask the brother that evening if we could be kept together.

I spared a thought for our Paddy again, as at least Alec and I had been together so far in this nightmare; poor Paddy was lost in the system somewhere facing the daily mental and physical battles totally on his own. I knew he would get through it, though, as Paddy was a real tough character who was mentally strong, and I just knew that we would one day be reunited. At least, I hoped we would, anyway.

The day seemed to just pass insignificantly, as all I could think of was our meeting with the brother later on and what I was going to say to him. I really did not want to upset him and make the situation worse, but I just had to try to find out what laid ahead of us next. Bedtime came around and the brother came to see Alec and I, as he had promised to do.

"So, Porter, what is it that you need to speak to me about?" the brother said in his somewhat unique harsh tone.

"I just wanted to ask you if me and Alec could be sent back to Bamber Bridge when the school closes here, as we were happy there?" I nervously enquired. I knew that the children's home in Bamber Bridge was not too far from Bootle, as we had previously escaped from there and made it back to our Granny Porter's house, although the old bugger turned us into the police when we did.

"We are worried about moving to a new school, Sir, so can we please stay together as we have always been together since they took us both away from our home after our mum and dad died. Can we please go back to Bamber Bridge?" I begged.

I could immediately see by his facial expressions that the Brother was not happy with my questions, and he sternly replied, "Porter, you will go wherever the headmaster and the school governors send you. You will be treated in the same way as every other boy at this school, and you will be informed of where you are going when the headmaster is ready to tell you."

He made sure that all the other boys in the dormitory heard what he had to say before swishing his cane against his cassock as he always did as he exited the dormitory on his little ego-trip again. I realised that there was no point trying to get any information from the Christian Brothers about where we may be sent, so I did not ask again.

Rumours and whispers were rife throughout the school during the following week or so. Boys could be seen gathering in the usual little groups, discussing various 'what if' scenarios and anxiety levels were clearly higher than usual. Boys told others of stories about various other Roman Catholic schools were they had been; most of these tales were quite scary, as nobody seemed to have anything good to say about any of these schools. They told of beatings and various other acts of cruelty that the Christian Brothers had dished out at these places. I was not sure if half of them were exaggerating, but I already knew what Alec and I had experienced, so I really wasn't expecting the next school to be a bed of roses.

During this period of uncertainty, the thoughts of escaping with my brother yet again raced around my mind every minute of every day. I could not bear to think about Alec not being with me, so I decided that we would try to escape again. We were in a home in Brentwood, and I did not have a clue where Brentwood was. I only knew that we were in Essex and that we were not too far from the south coast. Our home was in Liverpool in the northwest of England, so I knew that we had a little work to do if we were going to escape and get to the city we called home again. I did not say anything to Alec about my intentions at this stage, as I did not want him to worry, so I calmly went about my everyday life at the school whilst carrying out a reconnaissance mission in line with what would be our next plan to escape.

The brothers' living quarters were in front of the main entrance of the school, so escaping through the main entrance was not an option, as we would surely be caught. The school was surrounded by high walls, so I knew that such a bid for freedom with Alec in tow was going to be difficult. I was also far too aware that we would be severely punished if caught trying to escape, but I was desperate to get away from there. I knew that wherever we were sent next, whether it be together or on our own, it would result in us having to put up with lads trying to bully us and the cruelty of the Christian Brothers.

That Sunday morning, as usual, I went to the church to get ready to help Father Carl serve mass to the congregation. Myself and the two other altar boys dressed and waited in the room for Father Carl to return from smoking his pipe in the kitchen garden, which he always did before mass. I watched him as he came in. Father Carl took the key to the door that led to the kitchen garden from his pocket, locked the door behind him and placed the key on top of the doorframe before going on to enter the church.

I instantly knew that that key that he sneakily kept on top of the doorframe was the key to our freedom. Alec and I would need to somehow get here and sneak away through the door when the time was right. I felt a little bad as I knew that Father Carl, who was the only Christian Brother that I liked, as he was kind to us, would be disappointed in me once the alarm had been raised and they had discovered we had gone, but I soon set my feelings aside and continued planning. I knew the kitchen garden area very well, as I had worked there previously. There was a tool shed in the garden. I knew exactly what tools were in there, and I thought that we may be able to hide in this shed until darkness fell and then we would tackle the climbing of the boundary walls.

As the days passed by, I constantly pondered how Alec and I could successfully scale the high walls whilst carrying out my usual mundane school life.

There were no trees near the walls, so climbing a tree and jumping over was not an option. I thought and thought until my mind went blank, then suddenly I realised that if we broke into the tool shed and took a wheelbarrow and placed it up against the wall, Alec could help me get on top of the wall and then I could pull him up and over it. We could then run across the fields to the main road to the town (I knew the town was not far away, as the US troops had taken us there in their army trucks on that special Christmas Eve). I thought that we could hide in the town somewhere and then bunk a train back to Liverpool. The plan was officially hatched!

The next day, I told Alec about the plan and he looked at me nervously, as he knew what we could expect of we got caught. I explained that we could be separated at the move, so he soon agreed that we must try to escape and get home to Liverpool again. We had been together all of our lives and simply could bear not being together, so this was a chance that we just had to take.

We decided that on Saturday morning, Alec would go to confession as usual and after he had finished I would then inform the brother in charge of the recreation room that I was going to help with the cleaning of the cross and other duties that we usually did in church on a Saturday morning. It was here I would wait for Alec before we made our bid for freedom.

Alec was to leave the confessional box and walk over and meet me in the church, by which time I would have I retrieved the key to unlock the back door from the top of the doorframe. I had seen Father Carl put the key there last Sunday before mass, so I knew exactly where to look for it. Alec and I went over this plan a few times just to make sure it would work, or so we hoped. The following Saturday was to be the big day, and we both had restless nights leading up to it.

Saturday morning arrived, and it was time to make a bid for freedom again. That morning, I remember that the sun was shining and the birds sang sweetly outside the window of our dormitory, as if they were wishing us luck. Alec and I completed the obligatory duties before heading down for breakfast. Neither of us could eat much at breakfast that day, as we were clearly anxious about the proposed escape plan and the consequences that would await us if we failed to get away. I had little doubt that the punishment would be severe if we got caught and that Alec would receive the same beating as I would if it went wrong. Despite this, we just had to take a chance. It was now or never.

After breakfast was finished, I went to the brother in charge of the dining hall and asked if I could go to the church and start my cleaning jobs before Father Carl began taking confession. I told him that I would go to confession after I had finished cleaning the candlesticks and the other items in the church and that Father Carl wanted the jobs done soon. The brother in charge did not suspect anything, and he let me leave the dining hall to go to the church.

Once inside, I began cleaning the candlesticks whilst the butterflies in my stomach seemed to do somersaults as I waited with a cold sweat for Alec to arrive. Alec soon joined me, and I told him that we would have to be quick, as I knew that the church was almost full with the other boys waiting to go into the little room with Father Carl and confess their sins.

I quickly reached up for the key, opened the door as quietly as was possible with the big old squeaky hinges that were on it, and we ran over to the tool shed in the church kitchen garden area. Our hearts were pounding heavily as we tried to get our breath back ready for the next stage of the escape.

"It's too late to turn back now, Alec. Let's go," I whispered as we crouched in the cover of the tool shed. Alec just looked back at me with fear in his eyes again.

We took a wooden wheelbarrow and ran with it as quickly as we could to the wall at the far end of the garden. I propped the wheelbarrow up on its wheel with the handles against the wall and I clambered up and balanced carefully on top of it in an attempt to reach the top of the wall. I managed to get hold of the tapered edge of the bricks, pulled myself up as far as I could without losing my grip and then Alec then stood on the barrow, pushing me up from below. I pulled myself up and was now balancing on the top of the wall with my stomach acting like an anchor.

"Reach up, Alec, and I'll pull you up here," I called to him.

My brother stood on the wheelbarrow and reached up for my trailing hands, but he fell off and clattered to the ground like a sack of potatoes.

"Hurry up, Alec. Try again. Come on!" I said.

I knew our window of opportunity for escape was closing...and closing fast. Alec jumped up and got on to the wheelbarrow again and as I reached down to him once more, I saw one of the brothers running down the path towards us.

"Stop there, Porter!" yelled this very irate brother as he hurtled towards us.

His face was like thunder.

"Quick, Tommy. They're coming," Alec cried.

I managed to grab Alec's hands and summoned all of my strength to pull him up the wall to me. I guess desperation and fear increased the strength of our grip, but just as I had pulled Alec close to the top of the wall, the angry brother had grabbed hold of his ankles. The tug of war was on. The brother pulled Alec's legs with all of his might and I pulled his arms with mine. Poor old Alec was caught in the middle, but we would not let go. The brother's strength and weight proved victorious in this tug of war, and we soon came crashing down from the wall.

Alec was sprawled out on the grass and I had fallen on top of the brother, who was not amused. The fact that I landed directly on top of him and knocked him to the ground in a heap clearly multiplied his level of anger. I was unaware of my landing pad, as I must have clipped my head on the wheelbarrow whilst falling and was now in a somewhat dazed state. I saw stars flash before my eyes and I felt a warm sensation spreading from my head down my face. My clash with the wheelbarrow on my rapid descent from the top of the wall had resulted in a nasty cut to the head that was bleeding like a pig at slaughter.

When my head stopped spinning and the stars in front of my eyes disappeared, I realised that the brother who had initially caught us and pulled us down, now had me in a headlock. I could see several brothers at the scene now, one of whom was gripping Alec by the neck and violently slapping my brother hard around the face and head.

"Leave him alone," I screamed. I kicked and wriggled like a madman as they dragged us back up the garden path, dishing out a flurry of blows on the way. I remember seeing some of the boys watching the commotion through the windows that overlooked the garden. We were taken to the church and the door slammed shut behind us.

We were flung towards the empty chairs in the room and told to sit down. The blood was still pouring from my head, so the brother who had pulled us down and who had dragged me up the path, then started to clean the blood off me and put a bandage on my head. "That was a very stupid thing to do Porter. You could have been killed falling off that wall onto the concrete path," the brother said sternly as he patched up my wound.

I yelled back, "If you hadn't pulled Alec down then we wouldn't have fallen off the wall!"

This earned me another slap across my face for my cheek.

By this time, Father Carl had entered the room and I could see by the look on his face that he was not happy. "Who opened the door?" Father Carl asked the other brother.

"It was Thomas Porter, Father Carl," the brother replied as he pointed at me and glared.

"Is this true?" Father Carl asked me.

I just nodded my head and put my head down as Father Carl took the key to the door, put it in his pocket and left the room in silence. I felt sad, as I liked and respected Father Carl, and I knew we had let him down and betrayed his trust.

Alec and I were soon on the familiar journey to the headmaster's office. I knew what was coming, and I felt sorry for Alec, as I felt that I had let him down, too. He was now in for a beating and it had been my idea to escape first. I felt bad. I was first up as Alec stood in the corridor with the brother outside the headmaster's office whilst I went in.

"Porter, you are the most disruptive boy that has ever been in St Charles School," the headmaster shouted angrily. "Why do you keep trying to run away? You have no family and nobody wants you and your brother. We are the only family that you have, so the sooner you learn that, the better it will be for you."

I tried to explain why we had tried to run away and that it was my fault and nothing to do with my brother, but as it always did, my words fell upon deaf ears and he totally ignored me.

"Give him six strokes with the cane on his backside," the headmaster snarled to the brother who had accompanied me.

I was taken to another room, told to take my trousers and pants down and made to bend over a desk humiliatingly again while the brother dished out the punishment with no mercy. I could hear Alec crying out with pain from the next room as he received the same. I wish

I could have taken his punishment for him, as it was all my fault.

We were then taken back to the dormitory with our sore backsides and bruised bodies and told that we would have to stay there all weekend and that we would not have any recreation time whatsoever. Our meals were brought to us by other boys, and we spent most of the time crying whilst we sat on our beds nursing our sore backsides. We could both hardly sit down as a result of yet another bout of lashings with the cane.

At mass on the Sunday, Alec and I had to sit between two of the brothers, each of whom watched our every move. I felt like a prisoner again. Once mass had finished, it was straight back to the dormitory. Later that day, whilst all the other boys were having recreation time, the door to the dormitory swung open and we saw the brother in charge, accompanied by Father Carl. The brother was told to leave the room by Father Carl, who then sat on my bed with me.

"I am very disappointed in you, Thomas. You have betrayed my trust," Father Carl said as Alec and I began to cry.

"You told lies when you said you were going to the presbytery to help with the duties of an altar boy, when really all you were doing was attempting to run away. I thought you liked being an altar boy, Thomas, and your behaviour had been improving, so why did you do this?"

"The reason we tried to run away, Father Carl, was because we are going to be separated and sent to different schools," I replied as my eyes filled up with more tears.

"We have always been together since we were first taken from our family. We only have each other."

"Why did you not tell me about what was worrying you both? I am sure that the headmaster and the school governors will try to keep you both together, as you are so close. They have always done so," Father Carl said.

Father Carl reassured us that he would speak to the Headmaster and the Bishop when he next saw them on the coming Sunday. He told us he would do his best to see to it that we were not sent to different schools when St Charles School closed.

"I want you to continue to serve mass with the other boys, Thomas, for the final mass. The bishop will be in attendance that day, so let's show him what a good boy you really are," said Father Carl.

"Thank you very much, Father Carl. I promise that we won't try to run away again and I'll see you next Sunday at mass. Goodbye," I replied as Father Carl left the dormitory.
I felt a little better, as Father Carl was a good man and I knew he meant it when he said he would do his best for us.

A few days after the failed escape attempt, as we were sitting in the dining hall eating breakfast, the headmaster came in, demanded silence and explained that he was to read out a list of names of the first batch of pupils who were going to be transferred the following to a different school. I felt sick to the stomach, a cold sweat rushed upon me and my heart started thumping so fast in my chest cavity that it felt like it was going to leap out onto the dining table as I waited to hear our names being called out.

The headmaster read out the list of names to the hall full of boys who all waited eagerly to learn of their next school. To our relief, neither of our names was called out that day, so we were still together until the next roll call, at least. The boys whose names had been called out stayed behind after breakfast and the others left the dining hall. One of the boys who had sat on my table was on the list, so we said a quick goodbye and he wished us luck.

The next morning soon came around and there we were again in the dining hall as the headmaster came in to announce another list of departing pupils. He said that these pupils would be going to a school called St Joseph's. Alec was sitting alongside me and immediately clutched my sleeve as the headmaster began to share with us the contents of his list. Alec's name was read out and when I looked at him, he had the look of fear in his eyes. He held my sleeve tightly and we both sat nervously, praying for my name to be included in the list.

Every time a name was read out, Alec and I looked at each other and he seemed to look paler and paler with every name. My insides were twisting as I desperately waited for to hear my name. The roll call went on for what seemed like a week and just as it sounded like the headmaster was finishing his communication, the words "Thomas Porter" were called out. Alec and I hugged each other so hard that we nearly fell off the bench. Tears of relief ran down our cheeks. I did not care where the hell they were going to send us now I knew we were going to be together – that was all that mattered to me. I never found out for certain, but I am sure that Father Carl had something to do with us being kept together, or at least, I would like to think so.

Breakfast ended and we stayed behind with the other boys whose names had been called out. There were four boys from my table, so at least we all knew each other, which made us all feel better about the move to St Joseph's. One of the brothers who had been given the duty of ensuring that the move went according to plan, then came over to us and took us back to the dormitory. He informed us that the next morning we were to empty our lockers, fold up all of our clothes and put them into baskets that would be provided for us. We were then to strip our beds, fold the sheets, roll the mattress up and place it at the head of the bed with the folded sheets placed on the foot of the bed.

I remember lying in my bed that evening thinking about my time in St Charles School and wondering what the next school would be like. Again, I wondered about what had happened to my brother Paddy and where he may be, as I knew Paddy would be on his own through this nightmare. I just hoped that he was getting through it. I missed all of my family so much and I hoped that we would one day be together again before I closed my eyes and went to sleep that night.

The next morning, our dormitory prefect eagerly ensured that the instructions given to us by the brother the day before were followed to the letter. We all stripped our beds and folded the sheets and mattress before the brother arrived to take us to the clothing room, where we collected the clothes that we were to travel in. We then returned to the bathroom, where we washed before putting on our travelling attire. The brother took us to the recreational hall to wait for the headmaster.

The headmaster eventually arrived, accompanied by two brothers who stood alongside him like accomplices, as they so often did. He told us that these two brothers would accompany us to the new school. The headmaster then called each of our names out and as each name was called, we had to step forward for him to inspect each of us and say a few words.

"Thomas Porter," called the headmaster. I stepped forward for inspection and I wondered what he would have to say to me. Would he say anything pleasant on my last day at St Charles?
"Porter, I hope you learn to behave, or your life will be hard," said the headmaster in his usual serious manner before turning to the next boy in line.
I was going to miss him like I would miss having the measles.

We were then all led in single file and in silence through the corridors to the front of the school and out to the bus that was waiting for us outside. Once we were all seated on the bus and we finally got the other side of those main gates, I shouted to the brothers, "Where are we going?"
"You'll find out when we get there," was the answer.

That was the last time I ever saw St Charles School in Brentwood, Essex.

Chapter Eighteen

Where Next?

Alec and I took our seats at the very back of the bus. We were joined by the other boys who had been on my table in the dining hall when I was prefect. Our little group had bonded during our time at St Charles School, but this didn't stop my mind racing about what was in store for us at our next destination on this bizarre journey of my life to date. There were six of us in all from my table at St Charles, and we all agreed that we would stick together at the new place and that we wouldn't put up with being bullied by anyone. I knew that they would look to me to look out for them and to sort out any trouble, as I had done whilst they were on my table previously. I put on a brave face and didn't show that this was playing on mind a little and that I was as nervous about going to this new place as they were.

The other boys on the bus overheard our conversation about sticking together to show a united front with any potential bullies, and in no time at all, they were also congregating at the back with us. One of the brothers from the front of the bus came down to the back and said in a harshly inquisitive manner, "You lot. What are you all talking about?"

Nobody spoke and all eyes looked at me, so I felt obliged to answer on behalf of the group. "We are just talking about the new school and wondering what it will be like," I said.

"If you behave yourselves, Porter, then things will be fine. If you do not, then you know what you can expect," he growled back at me.

I was hoping that he would tell us where the new school was, but he did not, so I just sat with my head pressed against the window of the bus as it trundled along, whilst I hoped in my heart that I would see a road sign for Liverpool.

That sign never appeared; I almost knew it would not. I knew that we were in the south of England. I knew Brentford was in Essex, as I had studied the map of the Great Britain at every opportunity at school. I really enjoyed looking at maps and could point out every part of the British Empire on a map at that stage of my life. As the miles passed us by, my mind wandered yet again and I thought of my family and my home in Bootle. I saw a sign that read 'London 15 miles', which underlined the fact that we were travelling further away from Liverpool. This made me sad, and I fought back a tear as my head rattled against the window of the old bus.

After a while, the bus pulled into a service station and the brothers told us that we would be stopping to use the toilets. We were told that we were to go in, accompanied by a brother, in groups of four. Alec was not allowed to go into the service station with me, so we went in separate groups. Obviously they thought that we might try to leg it again if we went in together. As if we would.

Once the toilet duties were finished, we were all given our packed lunches to eat before we set off again on our journey to St Joseph's School.

The nervous tension between the boys on the bus was building as the journey continued and it was not long until I saw a sign saying Orpington 10 miles. We went through what seemed to be large towns before we came to the sign that said Orpington. As we passed this sign, one of the brothers stood up at the front of the bus and said,
 "Be quiet! We are nearly there, so get all of your things together, as we will be getting off the bus soon."

The brother sat down and there was an eerie silence amongst us boys. Everyone's eyes bulged as they scanned the surroundings through the bus windows. The bus turned off the main road and I saw a big sign that read, 'St Joseph's Roman Catholic School For Boys'. The bus crawled up the long, tree-lined, drive towards the massive red brick building with huge windows at its front and a church at its side. The bus went through the large front gates of the school before stopping at the bottom of the steps that led to the front doors. We had arrived at St Joseph's Roman Catholic School for Boys.

As the bus driver brought the bus to a halt, I saw five serious-looking Christian Brothers dressed in black standing in line at the top of the steps. The sight of our welcome party sent a shiver down my spine. We were then ordered off the bus, and collected our belongings before following one of the brothers up the steps and through the large wooden doors of the school. The other brothers did not crack a welcoming smile, or even say a word. They simply stood there glaring at us as we walked past them. Here we go again, I thought to myself.

Once in the school building, we heard the sound of boots clomping up and down on the old wooden block flooring of the long wood-panelled corridors. The brother led us in silence through more doors and down a long corridor into a large room with a variety of holy paintings hanging from the oak walls. There was a large stage area in the room, which made me realise that it was the recreation room. We were all told to stand in a row facing the stage and there was a deathly silence in the room. I hoped Alec would not try to tug my sleeve to get my attention, as this was definitely not the time or the place.

After we had been standing in silence for five or ten minutes, the door of the recreation room creaked open behind us and three brothers walked in and made their way up on to the stage. The first brother who spoke to us was a little chap with white hair.

"Welcome to St Joseph's School, boys. My name is Brother Peter, and I am the headmaster here," he said in a surprisingly soft voice. "I know you must be feeling a little nervous about coming to a new school, but please do not worry too much, as we run a good school here. My door is always open if you ever need to speak to me. You will have to ask the brother in charge permission first, of course, but I will do everything I can to help you settle in here."

Now I was confused! I was not expecting such a friendly tone. The new arrivals looked at one another, as the headmaster in the previous school had never spoken to us in such a friendly manner. We weren't used to it. The other brothers went on to read the rules of the school out to us and as expected, they stressed that every rules must always be obeyed by all of us. The headmaster then said that we would all be placed together on the same dining table until we had settled in and had got to know the other boys at the school.

Names were then called out and classes and dormitory places were confirmed. My name was soon called out and the butterflies in my stomach awoke again, as I expected to be reprimanded. To my surprise, the reprimand never came, and I was treated like all the others. I was happy that I did not get singled out on my first day at St Joseph's School, and I was hopeful about this place. I was so relieved when Alec's name was also read out and I learned that we were to be placed in the same dormitory as each other here.

The headmaster then introduced us to Brother John , who escorted us to the laundry room to collect our new clothes. Our clothes were much the same as they had been at the previous school; that is, one set of everyday clothes and another best set for Sundays. Time was taken to ensure that this set fitted us and I remember feeling really smart when I tried on the Sunday best. I thought I would try to make a good impression, so I asked Brother John, "Is it just on a Sunday, Brother John, that we would wear our Sunday bests?"

"On Sundays, holy days and when we go on walks," Brother John replied.

I looked at Alec in amazement. We had never been taken on walks before.

Next stop was the dormitory. Brother John told us that we were not to make any noise whatsoever when we were walking inside the building, so we again followed him in silence as we made our way through the corridors to our dormitory. As we followed Brother John up the wide and ornate wooden staircase, one of our group broke the silence and began laughing about something or other. As he did, a voice like thunder bellowed from above: "Quiet, you lot."

We instantly lifted our heads and saw a short, fat brother with a head like a turnip standing at the top of the staircase, slapping his cane against his cassock. His face was as red as a beetroot and he did not look friendly or welcoming.

"These are the new boys from St Charles School, Brother Dominic," said Brother John before he left us with this man.

Once we had reached the top of the staircase, us newcomers then stood in a row outside the door to the dormitory, with this short, fat, angry Brother Dominic standing in front of us waiting to bark more orders at us on his little ego trip,

"I am Brother Dominic and I am in charge of the dormitory," The little man growled at us.

"You will, always, obey my instructions. Is that clear?" We all nodded to him in agreement.

"Any boy who does not obey my instructions will be dealt with by me. Understand?" he added as he swished his cane through the air fast enough to make that now familiar whoosh sound.

All eight of us nodded in silence.

Brother Dominic began making his way down the line, asking each of us our names as he checked us off on his list before telling each boy which bed number had been allocated to him. I was standing at the end of the line with Alec next to me. When Brother Dominic got to Alec, he stood right in front of him and put his face right in Alec's and asked, "Your name, boy?"

"Porter, Brother Dominic," Alec politely replied.
"Thomas?" Brother Dominic asked.

"No, that's Tommy there," Alec said quickly as he pointed nervously to me.

Brother Dominic gave Alec his bed number and quickly moved on to me as he began to slap his cane against his leg.

"So, this is the one that causes all the trouble, is it?" he said. I tried to tell Brother Dominic that it was not always my fault that I had been in trouble in the past, but before I could get my words out, he snapped and raised his cane to the underside of my chin and shouted, "Shut up, boy. You will speak when I tell you to. Do you understand?"

I nodded my head in agreement. It was at this point I noticed a distinguishing feature of Brother Dominic's face – one that would fascinate me for the duration of my time at St Joseph's School. Brother Dominic had a mole on his face that would get redder the angrier he became. I found this to be a great warning signal that allowed me to gauge the expected anger as he waddled towards us. It also made me want to laugh out loud at him, although I had to fight that particular urge on the grounds of health and safety (mine)!

I knew Brother Dominic was going to make my life hard at St Joseph's School and thought it was best to try to avoid him whenever possible. After he had given us our bed numbers and reeled off the dormitory rules (which were much the same as they had been at the other schools), another brother came into the room and whispered something to Brother Dominic. The spot on his face pulsated red again. He called a boy from the shower room to come and supervise us whilst we put our clothes away tidily in the lockers and made our beds, before he waddled off in anger, slapping his cane against his leg again. He looked like he was going to dish out some punishment to someone.

The boy who had been given the task of supervising us in Brother Dominic's absence was an Irish lad called Mick Kelly. He seemed really nice, and when we had finished putting our clothes away and had made our beds, he inspected them and helped us to rearrange things to make sure our work met Brother Dominic's standards. Mick explained the drill for showering and laundry days, as every dormitory had different days for the change of bedding and clothes.

"What's it like here, mate?" I asked Mick Kelly, as the other boys stood and waited to hear what Mick had to say.

"It's not too bad if you do as you're told. For God's sake, keep on the right side of Brother Dom, as he is the worst for dishing out the cane whenever he can. Oh, and don't call him Brother Dom, whatever you do!" Mick replied.

It was not long until Brother Dominic returned to the dormitory and inspected the beds and lockers. He grumbled and mumbled to himself whilst doing so.

"Do any of you piss the bed?" Brother Dominic snarled. There was silence again and we all knew that there would be a punishment for any bedwetting. "Kelly, take them down to the recreation hall and wait for the dinner bell to ring," said Brother Dominic.

Mick took us newcomers down to the recreation hall, and the other new boys walked behind me as we went in. I didn't mind, as we had pledged on the bus to stick together, and I was prepared to try to look after them if necessary. Three of the lads had been on my table at the previous school, and I had looked after them there, too. At the recreation hall, we were met by the brother in charge, who spoke to us politely and explained the rules of the hall. The man told us not to worry, as we would soon get to know the other boys in the school. This made me feel a little better about the place.

The brother in charge of the recreation hall then left, which led to all the boys who were in the hall crowding around us newcomers. Questions were fired out to us: "What was it like at your last school?"; "Where do you come from and how are you here?" The questions from the inquisitive natives soon passed, and out little group felt happy to continue to stick together with myself as the unelected leader of the group.

We heard the familiar sound of a dinner bell and joined the others in moving to the dining hall. As expected, there was a brother on the door of the dining hall waiting for us. He pulled our little group to one side and introduced himself as the brother in charge of the dining hall.

"I am going to keep you all together at mealtimes and I hope that you soon settle down here," he said. "Have any of you any experience of being a table prefect?" I remained silent, but Alec piped up, "Our Tommy was a prefect at St Charles School, Sir."

The other boys in the group confirmed this by nodding their heads to the brother, so he said to me, "Thomas, if you want to try it, then I will give you a month's trial to see how you behave."

I was happy to take on this duty, as I knew the boys well and it meant that we'd be kept together at meals, at least. The brother then nominated another one of our group as a prefect and we all took our seats at two tables next to each other in the dining hall and ate our meals, feeling content about our new surroundings and arrangements.

The rules of the dining hall at St Joseph's were very similar to that of previous schools I had been at, with one major difference. At St Joseph's, the brother in charge sat quietly at a table by the main door whilst we all ate, as opposed to him pacing the dining hall, shouting at everyone whilst swishing his cane angrily in the air. I was well impressed.

After we had finished our meal and cleaned up, Mick Kelly met us by the door as we were leaving and he asked us how we had got on and what the brother had said to us. I told him that we were happy, as we had all been allowed to sit together, and that he'd made me the table prefect. Mick came across as being a genuine person who seemed pleased for us. "That's a good start, Tommy as the brother is very fussy about the dining hall rules and who he chooses to be prefect, so well done, mate," Mick said. I was determined to try to do my best as a table prefect and to make sure all of us lads were okay.

Mick then took us from the dining hall back to the recreation hall, where he showed us the variety of activities that we could do to pass the time. These included playing cards, table tennis and a good selection of board games and puzzles. Our little group of newbies sat down and began to play cards, but as we did so, I noticed one lad who seemed to be just walking around the hall with a little crew of followers, spoiling the games and activities of the other lads. I had clocked this potential bully and his little gang of helpers, and it was not long before they made their way to our table.

The lad who appeared to be the leader of this little clique pulled up a chair directly opposite mine and just sat there staring at me. At first, I tried not to make eye contact, as I really did not want to start getting into trouble at St Joseph's, but this tactic didn't last long as there was no way I was going to be bullied. I soon stared back at him, and the atmosphere became tense as we both now sat staring at each other in silence. As the tension grew, one of the boys mentioned that the brother was coming, and this boy and his accomplices walked away.

"Is everything well, Thomas?" the brother asked me.
    He had obviously clocked what had been going on and had come over to intervene.
    "Yes, brother. Everything is fine." I replied.

The brother then went over for what appeared to be a little word with this troublemaker.

"Who was that lad Mick?" I asked Mick Kelly.

"That is Smithy. He is a bully and you should try and stay away from him, Tommy, as he will get you into trouble with the headmaster," replied Mick.

So, that was my first meet with a boy that I would come to hate. Smithy.

We answered questions from the other boys, who were keen to know more about us. I did not really say much, as I just wanted to be left alone and get on with being in this place and to look after my brother Alec until we could find a way to get home to our family in Liverpool. It was the same routine as it had been for so long now: the bell went for bedtime, so off we all trotted to the dormitory and stood by our beds, before putting our pyjamas on ready for sleep time. I went to the large communal bathroom to have a wash before getting my head down.

To my surprise, the cubicle door of one of the toilets swung open as I was leaving the bathroom and it almost hit me as I passed. Out came the bully-boy Smithy, pulling his pants up as he was leaving the cubicle. My heart raced as I decided whether to smash his face into the cubicle door. I stood there and glared at him, waiting for him to start. I was ready. Surprisingly enough, Smithy was not so brave without his little group of bully-boys to back him up and he just put his head down and walked past me in total silence. I left it there and fought my urge to pay him back for the bullying he had obviously been dishing out to a large number of the boys in the school. He knew I wasn't scared of him now.

I went back to my bed in the dormitory and told our little group about my encounter with Smithy the bully in the bathroom. Some of the lads who had been in the school for some time overheard me and came over and told me to avoid Smithy and his gang. They said that they had seen this before and if they could not get to me, then it was likely that they would try to pick on someone close to me. We agreed to try to stay out of their way. I did not want Alec to become a target for their bullying and I certainly did not want any more beatings with the cane from the brothers, as the pain I had suffered from the last one for trying to run away was still fresh in my mind. I really wanted to try to behave at this new school to try and make life easier for both Alec and I.

After the lights had been turned off and I had been trying to get to sleep for an hour or so, I needed to go to the toilet. I knew that I would have to walk past the beds of Smithy and his gang to get to the toilets, so I did so whilst being on my guard. The small night light at the end of the dormitory was the only light and I could see Smithy rocking from side to side in his bed as I approached. My eyes were opened wide, with my pupils trying to take in as much light as possible. When I got closer to his bed, I saw that he was sleeping and thought that he must have been having nightmares or something, with the way in which he was now tossing and turning in his bed. When I returned to the dormitory, Smithy was still wriggling about in discomfort, so I walked past as quietly as I could with a smug grin on my face. I later learned that he did this every night. So that was my first day over with at St Joseph's Catholic School For Boys, and I eventually fell asleep after thinking of all of my brothers and sisters and where they may have been. It was a familiar dream.

The next morning seem to come quickly. We all got washed and dressed and went for breakfast in the recreation hall. The new boys were told to stay behind after breakfast to be addressed by the headmaster. The headmaster, accompanied by three of the brothers, then told us which classes we were to attend. Alec was in a different class to me, but I was not bothered, as we knew that we would meet up at every break time and would sit together at every meal.

The headmaster also went to say that we would all be expected to work at the weekends and that we would receive 2/6 per week as wages. The payment would be kept in our account and when we had enough, we could then spend the money in the school shop to buy items such as sweets and comics. He also said that some boys who were on "free walks" could even spend their money in the shops in the nearby town. "Free walks"... I just had to ask what this was all about.

The Headmaster told us that if the weather was favourable on a Sunday, some boys who had worked well and who had been behaving themselves, would be taken out on walks by the brothers, and they could spend their pocket money. He went on to say that we would not even be considered to go on these "free walks" for at least a month, as us newcomers would need to earn their trust first. I immediately looked at Alec and we both smiled in excitement. Neither of us had really spent much time outside of the children's homes since we had been taken away from Liverpool. It seemed that life would be better at this school, hence our smiles.

When the headmaster mentioned work, I assumed that I would be given a job in the gardens, as that is what I had done previously. I was pleasantly surprised when I was allocated work in the sports room, where all the sports equipment for the school was kept. It was my job to make sure that all the dirty football kits were put into the laundry baskets, ready to be taken to the school laundry. I was also responsible for making sure all the football boots were clean and were stored correctly in the boot lockers.

Alec was given the job of cleaning the main hall and the large ornate wooden staircase of the school. He was to help the other boys in his team to wash the floors before buffing them to a shine with a makeshift buffer. This was a hard job, as the buffing tool that Alec and the other boys had to use was made up of a square wooden block with a cloth on it, attached to a long wooden handle. They would spend hours pulling and pushing this thing until the floor sparkled every weekend.

The headmaster told us that the school had an excellent reputation for being good at sports, and that we were all expected to play an active role in such activities. Later that day, we met with Brother David who was the sports master of the school. He asked each of us what sport we wished to take up. Alec picked football and running and I said football and boxing. Brother David told me in no uncertain terms that they did not do boxing at St Joseph's, so football would have to do for me. As time went by, Alec got chosen to represent the school again at cross-country running, but I never even had the chance to practice. With hindsight, I wonder if they had been aware of my capers at the cross country at St Charles School previously.

Time seemed to pass us by, and both Alec and I settled in well at our new school. I was trying my hardest to stay out of trouble, but there was tension when I came face to face with Smithy with his little gang of bully-boys in tow. He would glare at me, and I would simply glare back. I really hoped that he would just leave Alec and I alone, as I was desperate to be given the chance to go out of the school on one of the "free walks" the headmaster had told us about on our first day. Deep down, I knew that a fight with Smithy was sure to happen one day, but I really wanted to stay out of trouble at St Joseph's.

Things appeared to be going well for Alec and I. The school had four football pitches, as well as a grass running track. Alec and I managed to get picked for the school football team, and I remember trying to emulate (without much success, I may add) my footballing hero, Nat Lofthouse. Nat Lofthouse was the centre forward for England at the time, and I had seen his photograph in a football magazine. Sometimes we played against teams from other schools. We always played at home, as away matches may have resulted in escape attempts. Life seemed to get a little better. I was managing to stay out of trouble and despite a few instances of arguing that escalated to pushing and shoving, there were no real fights to report.

After tea on a Saturday, the priest would hear confessions in the church, which was situated within the school grounds. Every class would take its turn and pupils would make their confessions on the Saturday so that they could then receive Holy Communion on a Sunday. Confession was a strange old event. Pupils would be escorted to the church by a couple of the brothers and we would then sit in silence awaiting our turn to go in to the confession box and tell our sins to the priest who would be sitting on the other side of the black curtain.

Although it was a little odd, I felt better once I had been to confession and told my sins (and believe me, there were a few) to the priest. The priest would then give a penance to say a few 'Our Fathers' and loads of 'Hail Marys' at the altar rail. It was always whilst kneeling at the altar rail that I would feel sad and lonely. I would start to wonder what may have become of my brothers and sisters and I wondered if they were happy or if they were feeling sad like I was. I would always end up praying to God to ask him to let me see them again one day soon.

One day, whilst we were all sat at our tables in the recreation hall, the headmaster came to our table and told us all to wait there for him, as he needed to speak with us after food. I racked my brains to think if I had done anything wrong, but could not think of anything. Food came and went and the headmaster, Brother Peter, appeared at our table once more.

"I want to talk to you all about two matters," the headmaster said to us all as we sat there in anticipation of what he was about to tell us.

"First, I must congratulate you all, as I have been told by our brother in charge of the dining hall that he is pleased with your behaviour. As a result, I would like to confirm that Thomas Porter is now officially promoted to prefect of this table," he added.

I was so pleased and felt proud to have been given the role of prefect. This was the best news I had received for quite some time, until the headmaster added, "As a reward for your good behaviour since you have arrived at St Joseph's School, I am pleased to tell you that you have been selected to go on the 'free walk' this Sunday afternoon. I must tell you, though, that if there is any bad behaviour between now and Sunday, then you will not go for the walk."

Wow! We were over the moon with excitement at this news. We could not wait for Sunday to arrive. I told the lads on our table not to talk too much about it when we got back to the dormitory, as certain others may try to spoil things for us in the meantime.

After dinner on Sunday afternoon, our group lined up in two orderly lines outside at the front of the school building with big, beaming grins on our faces. We were so excited at the prospect of going out of the school for the afternoon. Brother Peter laid down the law, as was expected, and reiterated the need for each of us to represent the school to the required high standard whilst we were out. He then went on to call our names out individually and we were given 2/6 that we could spend whilst out on the walk. He explained that any money not spent would have to be returned to him after the walk, and that he would see to it that it went back into our accounts.

The two lines of boys, headed and followed by one brother at the front and one at the rear, then made their way down the driveway of the school, crossing the main road before following the pavement all the way in to the nearby town of Orpington. We were all dressed in our Sunday best clothes and looked with open mouths in the windows of almost every shop that we passed. It had been an eternity since Alec and I had seen a shop; the last time being on Marsh Lane in Bootle. We hurried into the first sweet shop that we came to and bought some sweets to munch on that afternoon.

I remember seeing a shop called Woolworths and was astounded by how many items it contained. It seemed to sell all sorts of things, and I could have spent hours in there, I reckon. Any money that we had left was spent in Woolworths that day. I remember one of the boys bought toothpaste in a tube – that's right…in a tube! We had only ever used toothpaste from a tin, so this was a real novelty. One of the other boys bought a jar of Brillcream for his hair. Again, I had never even seen Brillcream before, and it was not long until several of us took dollops of the cream to style our hair. I remember the brother laughing at us, saying that we'd have a job to get the Brillcream out of hair tonight before bed.

We then took our new hairstyles to a nearby park, where we played on the swings. I saw some older boys from our school who appeared to be in the park on their own. They came over and began talking to the brothers who accompanied our group. I thought this was strange, as they were on their own and the brothers did not seem to be telling them off or anything. We carried on playing in the park for quite some time before the brothers called us together, counted us and began to take us back to St Joseph's. On the way back, I asked one of the brothers why the boys in the park were on their own and were not walking back to the school with us.

"Thomas, those boys are on 'free walks'. They are all boys who will soon be 15 years of age, which is the age they will be leaving the school," the brother informed me.

This conversation with the brother sparked a question that I had never, ever asked myself: how old is Tommy Porter? I genuinely did not know how old I was at that point. I could never recall having a birthday, and had never even given it a moment's thought until then. I could not wait to get back to school to find out exactly how old I was and the butterflies in my stomach began to flutter again as we walked.

Once we arrived back at St Joseph's, those of us who had any money left gave it back to the brother in charge. Alec and I did not return anything, as we had blown the lot on our afternoon of relative freedom. Just before we were to be sent back to the dormitory, I plucked up the courage to ask Brother Peter, the headmaster, the question that had been burning on my lips every step I had taken on the journey back to school. I felt stupid asking, but I just had to know.

"How old am I, Sir?" I asked sheepishly.

The headmaster looked at me strangely and replied, "Why do you ask this, Thomas?"

"I want to know when it will be time for me to go on 'free walks', Sir. How old am I now, Sir?" I asked again.

"I will check the records and let you know tomorrow after dinner. Now, go and get changed," the headmaster replied.

I could not wait for the next day to come, as I desperately wanted to know how old I was. I didn't mention anything to Alec, as I didn't really know how to tell him that we did not know how old we were. I also did not want him to start worrying that I may leave one day before him.

Monday came and went with the usual boring maths lesson. The day started as any Monday did; that is, with us stripping our bedclothes and exchanging them at the laundry room for clean ones for the week, before making our way to breakfast. Mondays were particularly tedious. I found it hard to concentrate in lessons this day as my mind raced with the need to know how old I was.

Dinnertime came, and I waited at the table after food had finished and tables had been cleared. Alec was curious why I was waiting to see the headmaster after dinner, as opposed to our usual routine of going outside to play football. I assured my brother that we had not done anything wrong, but that I just needed to see the headmaster. Alec sat with me, intrigued to learn what for.

A short while after the other boys had left the dining hall, Brother Peter, the headmaster, entered the room and came over to us with a smile on his face. My stomach muscles wrenched with suspense.

"Thomas, you will have to wait a little longer before you can go for free walks. You will be 14 years old on the 23 September, and it is July at the moment," said the headmaster.

"I am very pleased with the way in which you have both settled down in the school. Please keep up the good behaviour," he added before leaving the room.

For the first time in my life, I now knew how old I was. I longed for the months to come and go, so I could go on those "free walks".

Chapter Nineteen

Summer Camp

The summer of 1954 was a good time for Alec and I. He was doing well, and enjoying running in his cross-country races, and I had became a regular member of the school football team. I loved playing football and felt great playing in the position of centre forward. After a few matches for the school, Brother David, who was in charge of the team, said that I was to then play as right back. I was disappointed, as I wanted to be like Nat Lofthouse, however, Brother David told me that I would change to play in defence if I wanted to remain in the team. He reckoned I was being too rough with the opposing goalkeepers and was getting my name taken by the referee too many times. It didn't look good on the school. Of course, I accepted and continued to play football for the school.

A few weeks after my conversation with Brother David about changing positions in the school team, we were all sitting in the dining hall when Brother Peter, the headmaster, came in and told us all to assemble in the recreation hall after our food. Again, my heart sank when I heard those words. Were we going to be told that were moving schools yet again? Would Alec and I get separated? The mood of the boys changed in the dining hall, and dinner was finished in an eerie silence.

After dinner, all the boys sombrely made their way to the recreation hall. Everybody wondered what the announcement was going to be about, and my stomach was doing somersaults again as we waited patiently for the headmaster. As the door of the recreation hall swung open to make way for Brother Peter to enter, you could have heard a pin drop. He swaggered on to the stage and said, "Boys, I have some good news." I am sure he must have heard a mass sigh from us boys as he went on to say, "St Joseph's School has been chosen to attend a summer camp on the Isle of Wight. The school is very lucky to have been invited to attend, as there were many other Catholic schools that had been considered."

"Where the hell is the Isle of Wight?" I whispered to Alec. He just grinned and told me to be quiet.

"I am delighted to have accepted this invitation and I am sure that every one of you will represent St Joseph's very well. Summer camp is to be held in the last week of August. If anyone misbehaves between now and then, they will not attend the camp and will remain in the school with Brother Dominic," he added, seeming to glance over at me in the front row.

Summer camp was two months away, and the thought of staying in the school with the horrible Brother Dominic did not really appeal to me (or to anyone else, for that matter). I had visions of Brother Dominic lashing out with his trusty cane, with his freaky pulsating spot on his head throbbing with anger as the other boys enjoyed fun and games at summer camp. Not a pretty sight at all.

"Further details of the summer camp will be disclosed closer to the date. It is now up to every one of you to prove that you can behave yourselves to go to the camp," the headmaster said before leaving the room to the applause of the boys.

I was determined that Alec and I would behave well enough to go to summer camp. It sounded great. Everyone left the recreation hall that particular time with big smiles and there was an atmosphere of excitement buzzing around the school.

In the forthcoming weeks leading up to summer camp, all the boys were clearly on best behaviour, including Alec and I. With hindsight, I wasn't sure if this was because everyone was so excited about the prospect of attending summer camp or if it was because they didn't want to stay on their own in school with Brother Dominic. Even my arch-enemy, Smithy, and his little gang of bully-boys did not give us any grief. They gave me dirty looks every time I saw them, but as long as they stayed away from Alec and I, then I was happy.

As the excitement about the prospect of attending summer camp gathered momentum, I recall asking Brother David, the sports master, whilst doing my allocated chores one day, "Brother David, what exactly will we be doing at summer camp?"

"Well, Porter, you'll all be competing in a tournament of track and field events and there's also a football tournament. Everyone will have to do their best, as we want our school to do well," he replied.

"Which school will the summer camp be held at, Brother David?" I asked inquisitively.

"All will be revealed closer to the date, Porter, so get on with your work," he said.

The more I heard about this summer camp, the more excited I became. I knew our school had an excellent cross-country running team, as it had won trophies in past competitions and we also had a half-decent football team, so I was sure we would do well for the school. I was quietly confident that I would be picked to play football, and Alec was a definite for the cross-country and other running races.

A week later, we were all told to assemble in the recreation hall as Brother Peter, the headmaster, wanted to talk to us about the proposed summer camp trip. The entire school sat on the floor in silence as we waited for the announcement to be made.

Brother Peter, accompanied by the two brothers who were responsible for organising the trip, entered the hall, stood on the stage and said, "The summer camp will be held just outside a town called Ryde on the Isle of Wight. It is to be held on a specially constructed site and you will be accommodated in tents for the week. The camp is to be held in the last week of August.

"We must all work hard, as there is still much organising to do between now and then, and some of you will be chosen to help with packing all the equipment that we need to take with us.

I am pleased to say that I have not had any reports lately of bad behaviour. Therefore, every one of you has earned the right to attend the summer camp. Well done. St Joseph's School has been chosen to attend as it has an excellent reputation that it has built up over the years, and it is up to you to maintain this reputation. Any boy who steps out of line and misbehaves will be severely dealt with," he went on to say before making his grand exit from the hall.

That night, every boy in the school went to bed excited. I managed to take a sneaky peek at my map in the dormitory to see where the Isle of Wight was. I was keen to seen how far from Liverpool the island was. My mind drifted off to the streets of Bootle again as my eyes grew tired and heavy, before finally going to sleep.

The next two weeks seemed to pass quickly. There were many meetings with the brothers responsible for organising the trip. As I was a table prefect, I was told that the boys on my table were to ensure that the cutlery and plates for the boys of St Joseph's School were washed and put away correctly after ever meal whilst at summer camp. I was to make a daily list of who had done what, which Brother David kindly offered to help me with. I was also expected to carry out my usual duty of helping with the football kit and equipment; making sure it was collected and placed in the laundry baskets after each game. I knew I was going to be busy, but this did not quell my excitement one bit.

The more information that was relayed, the more excited I became about the prospect of sleeping in a tent and getting out of the school for a whole week. The rumour that circulated was that we would all sleep in large tents, ten beds to each tent, and that we would be allocate a tent number on arrival. Brother David had told me that Alec and the other boys from my dining table would all be in my tent with me, so both Alec and I were happy with that. Result!

The day arrived for summer camp. It was a sunny Saturday morning and we all sat in the recreation hall, having packed what seemed to be masses of equipment, clothes and kits into large baskets that were stacked outside the main doors of the school. When our names were called, we loaded our own clothes onto the waiting buses and got on and took our seats. Then Brother Peter came on and said, "I must remind you of the importance of being on your best behaviour, and I wish you all a very happy camping trip."

The engine of the bus started and a cheer could be heard from the happy campers as the buses left the grounds of the school for summer camp. Alec and I had never been on a holiday, never mind a camping holiday. This was great. We did not know what it would involve, so we sat and listened to the some of the other boys who had been previously. We had been told that we would drive to Portsmouth, where we would then catch a ferry to the Isle of Wight. The only other time I had been on the water had been as a part-time stowaway on the ferries across the River Mersey.

Later that day, we arrived in Portsmouth and waited for the bus to drive on to the ferry. As we sat there, I gazed from the window of the bus at the large ships in the dock, just as they had been back home in Bootle. For a moment, I was lost in thought as the memories of the time I had spent with my family came flooding back. .

Once our bus had driven on to the ferry, we were let off in groups of four with a brother accompanying us. The ferry soon arrived at the Isle of Wight and we then made the hour or so journey to the camp.

When we arrived, the excitement on the bus peaked, as we were greeted with the sight of what appeared to be an army camp. It had rows and rows of tents with a huge tent in the middle. It looked like the circus tent that used to come to North Park in Bootle when I was younger, I thought to myself. The bus pulled in to the camp and we were allocated tent numbers. Ours was tent number 25, and all the boys from my table were to sleep there, we were told as we walked off the bus. I was reminded by Brother John that I was to make sure that everyone in my tent behaved during our time at the camp.

Our first task was to unload equipment and our clothes and, then carry our belongings to our tents. Once my group had arrived at tent number 25, we made our beds and then went headed for the shower block, where a brother was at hand to show us how to operate the showers. We were then taken to the big tent in the middle of the field. It was the biggest tent I had ever seen, and there were rows and rows of tables set out neatly in straight lines. My group was allocated table five, and we were again reminded that we would be responsible for making sure our own plates and cutlery were cleaned and put away after every meal. We had already agreed that we would take turns washing up, and we all knew who was to do what and when, so table five was organised.

After our tour of the dining tent, one of the brothers informed us that Brother Dominic would be inspecting the St Joseph's tents every morning to make sure that everything was as it should be. Our faces dropped, as we all knew that the fat, angry bully of a brother would be marching up and down our tents, slapping his cane against his leg and looking for an excuse to lash out at one of us. All the boys in the school seemed afraid of Brother Dominic, and we tried our best not to get on the wrong side of him.

Food time came and went that evening, and we were told that we were allowed to walk around the field unaccompanied, but that we were not to venture in to the surrounding fields, as they were for other schools. Everyone appeared to have enjoyed the freedom of walking in the field and the fresh country air in our lungs.

The first night in tent 25 was a happy one. The tent had no lights, but was partially illuminated by the lights that hung outside, and those in the shower block at the end of the row of tents. We all chatted happily about what we may do the next day whilst we lay in our make shift beds. The darkness of the night drew in, and Brother Dominic soon appeared in our tent on his nightly rounds.
"All talking must stop now. Any noise from any tent in the night, and the prefect responsible for that tent will be dealt with," he grumbled as he left the tent.

We all knew what he meant by this and as I was the prefect in charge of our tent, I made sure there was no noise from tent 25.

The next day, which was a Sunday, came and we awoke to glorious sunshine. After showering, we all made our way to mass, which was held in the dining tent. After that, I went to help my team sort the football kit and equipment for Brother David, as we had our first match the following day. Alec went off to the sports tent and met with the cross-country team and went on a training run in preparation for the competitions.

The week passed and it was great fun. My time had been spent playing football against other schools and our team managed to get as far as the semi-finals of the competition before it lost 2-1 to a side from a school in the Isle of Wight. Although disappointed, Brother John and David were pleased at our performance and behaviour on the pitch. Alec and the cross-country team also did well. They were placed third overall in the track and field competition.

On our final Friday evening, the night before we were set to leave camp and as we lay in our beds in tent number 25, we heard a commotion in the shower block. I asked the boy in the bed next to me what was going on. Apparently, some of the pipes in the shower block had been ripped from their fixings and the shower block had been flooded. The commotion appeared to be the voice of a very angry Brother Dominic, so this was not good news at all. This voice appeared to be getting closer and closer.

The door flap of our tent was flung open and in marched the somewhat irate Brother Dominic, complete with his pulsating spot on his head.

"Who is responsible for the damage in the shower block?" screamed Brother Dominic as he stomped down the tent towards my bed whilst swishing his cane angrily in the air.

"Is this your doing, Porter? he snarled as he banged his cane on my bed, which was near the entrance of our tent.

"No, Brother Dominic. I don't know anything about it." I replied.

Just as Brother Dominic raised his cane in the air, and I braced myself for what I thought was an inevitable beating, the flap of the tent flung open again. This time it was Brother John. Upon seeing Brother John enter the tent, Brother Dominic lowered his cane and turned to face him.

"What is the problem here, Brother Dominic?" asked Brother John.

"I am sure that Porter had something to do with the damage in the shower block," Brother Dominic replied.

"When did the damage take place?" Brother John enquired.

"Everything was fine when I checked the shower block before food, so it must have happened after then," Brother Dominic replied.

"Well, if that is the case, then it could not have been Thomas who did it, as he was with me and the other members of the sports team packing the sports equipment ready for the journey back to the school," Brother John said sternly.

Brother Dominic glared at me, shook his head and shouted, "I will find out who done this and they better look out," as he stormed out of our tent.

Brother John followed him out of our tent. I was glad he came in when he did.

Later that evening, we heard that the damage to the pipes in the shower block had been caused by some local boys who had managed to get on to the campsite. Brother Dominic was on patrol that evening, as he had been on every evening during the camp, and it was no surprise that he did not come into our tent to apologise for wrongly accusing me of the damage to the pipes. We knew what he was like and I am sure he would have been straight in to us if there were a chance to dish out some punishment, that's for sure.

Our final morning of summer camp had arrived and we got up, stripped our beds and went to the food tent for the very last time for breakfast. After we had filled our stomachs with a hearty meal, we returned to our tent to pack all of our belongings back into the baskets that had first brought them there.

The reality of returning to St Joseph's school hit me, and I wished the summer camp could have lasted a whole year. Lunchtime came and went, and the buses arrived. All of us boys loaded what seemed to be more baskets than we had initially arrived with onto the buses in preparation for the journey back to St Joseph's School. We stood in one big line and boarded the buses upon hearing our names being called out by the brother.

Our journey to the ferry began, and I remember looking around at the sad faces on the bus. Nobody wanted to go back to the school (apart from the brothers who had accompanied us on the trip). The brothers appeared to be happy with our sporting performances at the camp and also with our behaviour. That was my first experience of camping, and I'd thoroughly enjoyed it.

It was late on the Saturday evening by the time our bus arrived back at St Joseph's School. I remember seeing the headmaster, Brother Peter, waiting for us as the bus jolted to a halt outside the main doors of the school. We wearily carried our baskets of possessions and camping gear into the recreational hall before being addressed by Brother Peter.

"Did you have a good time at summer camp, boys?" he asked.

A big cheer that echoed around the hall followed before we told that we would be let off emptying the camping gear that evening, as it was late. We were told that we could leave it until after mass the next day. We returned to our dormitories, made up our beds and everyone seemed to fall asleep quicker than ever before. It had been a long day and a great summer camp.

Chapter Twenty

A Run-in with the Bully

After Sunday mass, all the equipment that we had taken to summer camp was unpacked a carefully put away. It was my job to sort all the football kit and to ensure that all the dirty kit was taken to the laundry. It was back to the routine of St Joseph's School again.

Later that day, the headmaster again addressed us all in the recreation hall. "You have done this school proud with your efforts and behaviour whilst at summer camp," he said. "Well, done boys. I have not received any reports of bad behaviour from any of the brothers."

I was so relieved to hear him say that as I was half-expecting to get pulled again for the damage to the water pipes that I knew nothing about. My group of friends hoped that it would get selected to go on another summer camp the following year. We had really enjoyed our time there.

Life at St Joseph's went on in the manner in which I had become accustomed. Some of the older boys had been informed that they were going to be allowed to leave the school. One of the leavers was to be my friend, Mick Kelly, and he told me that he was set to meet with the headmaster and some other people to discuss where he'd be going next.

I was interested to find out where Mick Kelly was going, as I knew that he had no family back in Ireland. I was worried about him, as I considered Mick to be a good friend to me, and I was going to miss him. Mick promised to tell me more once he had met with the headmaster and officials.

A few weeks passed by before Mick had his meeting. He came to my dormitory, sat on the bottom of my bed and told me, "I have been offered a place at a hostel in Hackney, in London, Tommy. They said they will try to help me to find a job in London."

"I'm going to miss you, Mick, but all the best, mate. I am sure you'll be OK," I replied.

"I've got nobody back home in Ireland, Tommy, so I've no choice, really, mate," Mick said.

Mick had always been kind to Alec and I, ever since we first met him and he helped us both to settle in to life at St Joseph's and showed us the ropes there. It was a few days before Christmas when Mick came in and told us he was leaving the very next day.

"I promise to come back and visit you here, boys, once I have settled into the hostel and started work," he said.

Sadly, I never saw Mick Kelly again. I often wonder to this day what happened to him when he left the school. Did he stay in London or did he return to

Ireland? I hope life turned out well for Mick, as he was a good friend to me during my time at St Joseph's.

It was Christmas Day 1954, and I remember waking in the dormitory being sad again, as I had done on the morning of every Christmas I'd spent away from my family. As happened in previous schools, some boys were taken in by local families over the festive period, but Alec and I were not fortunate enough to have been chosen. All the brothers would join us in the dining hall for Christmas Dinner after mass, of course.

It was a lonely time for Alec and I. My mind drifted back to the days when we spent Christmas with our family in Bootle, when Mum and Dad were alive. As children, we never got much in the way of presents at Christmas, but I guess it was because we had such a large family and times were tough and our parents simply couldn't afford presents for us. Presents didn't really matter, as I remember playing happily in the street and on Marsh Lane with all the other children. We made our own fun and loved making up new games to play, and we always had food on the table.

I envisaged my older sisters, Edie, Mary and Aggie, getting us younger ones washed and dressed ready to go to St James Church on Marsh Lane for Christmas Day mass. Alec must have seen that I was in a daydream, and he came over to my bed that morning and said, "Are you OK, Tommy? It's Christmas Day."
"I don't know where our brothers and sisters are, Alec, but I promise we will find them when we get out of

this place," I replied as the tears started to trickle down both of our faces.

The festive period passed without significance and life went on at St Joseph's. All was going well until one day a Brother David came to me one Saturday afternoon and said, "Thomas, your brother Alec has had an accident. He has fallen down the stairs in the main hall."

"What happened? How is he? Can I go to see him, please, Brother David?" I said as my head flapped with worry.

"Alec is with the nurse. You can go to see him, but you must wait outside the room until the nurse has finished with him," replied Brother David.

I ran as fast as my legs would take me to the sick room and as I arrived at my destination, Alec emerged from the room looking a little worse for wear. He had a cut on his head and a large bruise on his forehead.

"What happened, Alec?" I asked frantically.

Alec did not reply and just shook his head and the brother who was with him said, "It's okay, Thomas. He just has a small cut to the head. He slipped on some spilt water whilst cleaning the stairs. Take your brother to the dormitory for a lie-down, Thomas."

We arrived at the dormitory and I asked Alec again what had happened to him. He was upset, but told me that he had been cleaning the landing at the top of the main staircase of the school and Smithy and his mates began to mess around on the stairs below him. One of Smithy's bully-boys had kicked Alec's bucket of water over and water continued to spill down the stairs.

Alec would now have to start again and clean the stairs for the second time.

Alec had stood up to them and had asked why they had kicked the bucket of water over and Smithy had then pinned Alec to the wall and punched him hard in the stomach while his little gang stood behind him. Alec managed to wriggle free and tried to escape their clutches. As he did, Alec slipped on the water on the floor and he slipped head first down the solid wood stairs, much to the amusement of Smithy and his gang.

The two boys that had been cleaning the stairs with Alec had apparently and conveniently gone to empty their buckets when Smithy and his little gang arrived, intent on bullying my brother. After food that day, I went to find the two boys who had gone to empty their buckets at the time of the incident.

When I asked them what had happened, they said they did not see anything as they were emptying their buckets. I knew they were afraid of repercussions from Smithy if they told me anything. I knew that I had to sort Smithy out conclusively, otherwise he would pick on Alec again in the future and he may hurt him again. I was angry.

All I could think of was how I could get to Smithy whilst he was on his own. I knew that he was not so tough when he had no back-up and he wasn't the hard case that he made out to be. I decided that I would bide my time and wait until the night. I knew Smithy went to the toilet a lot during the night as I had clocked his nightly routine previously.

My plan was hatched and I would wait until the nighttime had drawn in. If no other boys were awake when Smithy went to the toilet during the night, then I would get him on his own and give him a good hiding. I was well aware of the risk I was taking, and the punishment that would be dished out by the sadistic Brother Dominic if I got caught, but he had to have it. It was now or never, and this bully had to be taught a lesson.

The evening drew to an end and we all retired to the dormitory. By the time I got to the dormitory, Smithy was already in his pyjamas and was sitting on his bed. As I went to the bathroom, I walked past his bed and stared at him. Smithy buried his head in a book and refused to make eye contact with me. It was just as well, really, as I think I would have pounced on him there and then and battered him in front of everyone if he had returned my glare. I had so much hatred in my heart for this guy. I hated bullies.

I went to the bathroom and waited angrily in a cubicle for Smithy to come in to the room in order for me to teach him a lesson. I waited and waited to no avail until Brother Dominic finally called for lights out. I returned to my bed and again Smithy avoided my eye contact. I nodded to Alec to let him know I was all right and to wish him good night, as I did every night. I had not told Alec or anyone of my intentions that evening.

Minutes seemed like hours as I waited for my chance to get Smithy. My mind raced and my blood boiled to the point whereby I was tired of waiting for an opportunity to arise. I knew that our lives in this place would be hell if this bully was not sorted out, so I waited no more. It was quiet in the dormitory and everyone appeared to be sleeping, so I carefully removed my bed sheets and climbed down out of my bed and then crawled like a soldier on my stomach past all the rows of beds until I came to Smithy's bed.

Smithy was rocking side to side in his bed, fast asleep. I looked around and saw his boots on the floor next to his locker. I grabbed one of his boots from the floor and pulled the sheet away from his face. This woke him up, but before he could raise the alarm, I smashed his boot into his face and grabbed him firmly by the throat. I put my face right into his and told him, "If you ever hit my brother again, I will kill you, you fat bastard."

He yelped, blubbered and said, "I'm sorry. Please don't hit me again."

Just as I raised his boot to smack him again, I heard a door slam closed down the corridor. I ran back to my bed, pulled the sheet over me and pretended that nothing had happened. It was just as well, as the unwelcome silhouette of Brother Dominic soon appeared.

Brother Dominic entered our dormitory waving his cane with a flashlight in his other hand.

"What was the noise I heard coming from this dormitory?" he yelled as he made his way to my bed.

Once he had reached my bed, Brother Dominic shone his flashlight into my face. My heart was thumping that much, I am sure he could hear it! I pretended to wake up and rubbed my eyes for authenticity.

"What's the matter?" I wearily asked him in an attempt to appear to have been sleeping.

The angry brother ignored me and he continued to walk up and down the floor between the beds. Everyone in the dormitory was now awake and you could have heard a pin drop. I broke out into a cold sweat as I waited for Smithy or someone to tell Brother Dominic what had happened and for the beating that was sure to follow. Much to my surprise, nobody said a word, including Smithy and the grumpy enforcer, who left the dormitory muttering, "If I have to come back here again, then you will all be in big trouble."

Later that night, I saw Smithy getting up and going to the bathroom. I resisted the temptation to give him another dig, but I did not get much sleep that night as I thought some of his mates might look to gain revenge. I was not proud of what I did to Smithy, but all the time that I had spent in these schools had taught me that I had to defend myself and my brother. This was just the way it was in the world we lived in. I look back and thank God that it was his boot that I grabbed, as I would have readily struck him with anything I could have laid my hands on that night.

The next morning came and those butterflies that seemed to have been in my stomach for quite some time again awoke and began to flutter when I heard a group of boys talking in the dormitory. They were talking about Smithy and the accident he had had in the bathroom late the night before. I walked past the group and past Smithy's unmade bed on my way to use the bathroom. Smithy was nowhere to be seen. Shit, I thought to myself

"Where the hell is Smithy?"

We went down for breakfast and I tried to act normally, so as not to have the fingers of suspicion pointed towards me. At breakfast, there was still no sign of the bully-boy Smithy, so I asked one of the boys who sat at his table, "Where is Smithy, then?"

"He has been taken to the sick bay because he fell in the bathroom last night and he has a nasty cut to his head," said the boy.

The nerves were jingling as I kept a straight face, although I was certain that I'd soon be taking a trip to the headmasters office very soon. I was sure that Smithy would report me to the nurse in the sick bay, but to my surprise, Smithy had been telling everyone that he had slipped during the night in the bathroom on a bar of soap that must have been left on the floor by someone. He was saying that he could not see the soap, as it was dark.

Despite Smithy apparently resisting the urge to get me in trouble, I was still convinced that the brothers would soon find out about my revenge attack on him. I was sure that a couple of the boys in the dormitory had heard or seen what had happened, so I could not relax. I ate my breakfast that morning and then started on my walk back along the corridor towards the stairs. As I approached the stairs, Smithy emerged from the sick bay accompanied by a Brother Dominic and sporting a large bandage to his head. This was it, I thought to myself. My mind's eye pictured Brother Dominic grabbing hold of me and beating me with his cane once I came within striking distance. Thankfully, we passed in the corridor without a word being said to me. Smithy did not look at me and Brother Dominic just waddled past me in his usual agitated style as my heart pounded hard in my chest.

I remember sighing to myself and was confused. I had expected Smithy to grass me up and to seek revenge, but to be fair to him, he stuck to his story and did not. I hoped his days as a bully were over and that we could both now just get on with life in the school. After lessons had finished that day, I met with Alec in the dining hall for food. We sat down and I told him what I had done.

"My God, Tommy, you could have killed him," Alec said when I told him.

"Did anyone see you do it?"

"Well, if they did, then nobody has said anything yet, Alec," I replied.

Alec and I ate our food as usual, and I asked the boys at our table what had happened to Smithy the night before. There was a noticeable silence before one of the boys said, "He slipped on a bar of soap in the bathroom in the night...serves him right." I felt better now, as I was certain that nobody was going to tell on me. I think most of the boys were glad that I had sorted the school bully out, and the incident was never mentioned again. I overheard one of the boys on Smithy's table saying to another, "Those Porter boys are mental, so stay clear of them."

My father always taught us not to look for trouble, but not to run from it either, if it found us.

Chapter Twenty-One

Wine and the Spider

Life at St Joseph's was much better than it had previously been. Many boys seemed to have left the school, with some going to live in hostels in preparation for life on the outside and some to live with their relatives. I was able to enjoy "free walks" and would relish the chance to walk into town without a brother by my side. At the end of every afternoon I was allowed out, I would always go to the park to wait for Alec. The supervised group of boys would always make its way to the park before returning to the school, so I would wait and walk back to school with my brother.

During one of these free walks, I met up with an older boy who had left St Joseph's to live in the hostel in Hackney earlier in the year. His name was Paddy Wall, and we chatted as we sat in the park. Paddy Wall told me that he had come back to Orpington to visit the school. As we chatted, I asked him what it was like at the hostel and if he had seen my mate Mick Kelly there, as Mick had promised to come back to visit me. I was curious to find out what this hostel was like, as it would probably be my home when I left this school.

Paddy Wall told me that the hostel was not a pleasant place at all. He said that there were all types of people living there, including drunks and thieves. He said that you could not leave any of your stuff there if you went out, as it would go missing if you did. Paddy Wall went on to tell me that my mate Mick Kelly had moved away from the hostel, although he did not know where he had moved to. Paddy told me that he was trying to find a room or flat somewhere else in London so he, too, could get out of the hostel as soon as he could.

As our conversation flowed, Paddy Wall enquired, "How is Smithy with his bar of soap?"

I was surprised that he knew about this.

"All the boys knew that you did a number on Smithy that night, Tommy. He was never the same after you sorted him out. Is he still at the school?"

I replied, "Smithy left about a month ago. He has gone to live with a relative in Bath, apparently. Things are better now, as the bullying seems to have stopped at the school."

I said goodbye and left Paddy Wall sitting in the park that afternoon. I have never seen him again to this day.

Some weeks later, a new priest arrived at St Joseph's Church in the school. His name was Father Simon, and he was quite young and seemed friendly. He wore a brown cassock that had a hood on it, so looking back, I assume he was a monk. Father Simon was always playing jokes on us boys, and he soon became popular.

One day after mass had finished, Father Simon informed us that he was going to start a woodwork class at the school and he asked if there were any volunteers to help him to prepare the room to set the class up. Myself and few others immediately volunteered, as it sounded like great fun. The next day after school, we went to the church, where Father Simon accompanied us to the large wooden door that led to the cellar. Nobody had ever opened this door, to my knowledge, so when the heavy old oak door creaked open and we saw the darkness that awaited, there were a few nervous gasps. Father Simon laughed and handed us boys a flashlight each to use.

Armed with our flashlights and Father Simon as back-up, we entered the room and made our way down the steps into the darkness.

When we shone the flashlights around, we were greeted with a room that was full of broken chairs and tables that looked as if they had been there for an eternity and seemed to be stacked from floor to ceiling. Our instruction from Father Simon before he left us to our own devices was to clear as much of the junk out of the room as possible. We were to remove the old furniture, complete with cobwebs, outside to the field by the side of the church.

The cobwebs rang alarm bells in my head as I was (and still am to this day) terrified of spiders, so I volunteered to stay by the doors and to carry the furniture out to the field once the others had carried it out from the deepest, darkest corners of the room. We all got stuck into our job and after a couple of hours of dusty, sweaty work, we started to notice that the room was a lot larger than we first thought and that its ceiling was made up of three large and rather ornate arches that obviously propped up the floor of the church above. It was then that Father Simon returned and congratulated us on our hard work, and he asked if we would help him again the following day. We agreed to do so, before heading off to get washed before food time.

After school the next day, out little team of helpers, which had been bolstered to five members with the addition of Alec, returned to see Father Simon at the church and continued with our task at hand. One of the boys asked Alec why I would not come into the room and Alec told him that I was scared of spiders. The leg-pulling began and I endured the expected taunts of being a wimp if I was scared of spiders. I insisted that I would carry the furniture from the doorway to the field and would not go in whatever they said. My so-called mates seemed to take great pleasure in shouting, "Look at the size of this spider," at every opportunity.

Beads of sweat ran down my forehead as I failed to see the comical side of things.

As we were busy clearing the dark cellar room of the church, Alec shouted to me, "Quick, Tommy. Come and see what we have found here."

Thinking this was just a ploy to get me in the room to look at a giant spider, I poked my head around the door and said, "No way am I coming in there. Stop bloody messing about and let's just get the job finished."

"No, Tommy. We are not messing. Come and see what we have found," insisted Alec.

I plucked up the courage and went into the dark room to see what all the fuss was about. Expecting to see some ancient gigantic spider that had ruled the room for the last 50 years, I was pleasantly surprised to find the boys holding what appeared to be old bottles with corks in them. There were boxes and boxes of the old bottles. Now I remembered seeing bottles similar to these in the cupboard in the church at St Charles School when I was a serving altar boy.

"I think they are bottles of wine. Put the bottles back into the crate and go and get Father Simon, someone," I said, before the temptation to open them got the better of us.

Father Simon appeared, and he was soon followed by the headmaster. They both thanked us for our good work and for reporting our find and sent us back to the recreation hall. Later that evening, both Father Simon and the headmaster came to see us in the recreation hall to thank us again for our hard work and honesty. Apparently, the wine had been used for communion quite some time ago, as the room had not been used for many years.

"Would you like us to help you move the boxes out of the room tomorrow, Sir?" I asked Father Simon.

He just smiled and said, "No, thank you, Thomas. The brothers will move the wine tomorrow to a safe storage place. I will make a note on the school records that you boys have done a good job here."

Tired after our toil, our team of cellar clearers relaxed on Alec's bed in the dormitory and talked about our day while we waited for lights out. My bed had been moved to right by the dormitory entrance. I was not sure if this made me the unofficial dormitory prefect or if it was so Brother Dominic could keep his eye on me in the nights. I quite liked the idea of being the prefect, and I was certainly not going to allow any bullying in my dormitory.

Anyway, as we were sitting on and around Alec's bed, one of the boys who had been helping clear the cellar with us went off to the bathroom. When he returned, he had a tin in his hand and he threw it on to Alec's bed when he got close. I thought it was a tin of sweets, as I had bought a very similar tin from the school shop a few days earlier. I made a grab for the tin and hastily opened it to get the first pick of the sweets. To my horror, the tin did not contain any sweets. Instead, it housed the biggest, blackest, hairiest bloody spider I had ever seen. The creature from hell jumped out of the tin and I jumped from bed to bed in a frenzied attempt to escape the room, to the sound of the other boys laughing at me.

As my escape drew closer and I had bed-hopped to what I considered to be relative safety from this giant arachnid, the double doors to the dormitory swung open and the familiar figure of a very angry Brother Dominic with his pulsating red spot on his forehead stormed in.

"Porter! What is this noise and what are you doing jumping on the beds, boy?" growled Brother Dominic.

I stopped in my tracks and he grabbed my arm tight with one of his chubby little hands and waved his cane menacingly with his other.

"The boys are chasing me with a spider in a tin, Sir," I said as my defence. Brother Dominic snatched the tin off Alec and shook it under my noise and hissed, "See, Porter? There is no spider here."

Alec joined in and said, "Sir, there was a spider in the tin. It must have dropped out onto the bed."

I shook like a leaf does in autumn waiting to fall from its tree. I was terrified. The spider was now on the missing list, along with Brother Dominic being on the warpath. This was not my idea of fun.

Brother Dominic marched me back to Alec's bed and he pulled the covers off the bed to try to find this spider. He wanted evidence. I just wanted the bloody thing killed! The bed covers went back, but there was no spider. Brother Dominic then flicked the pillow off the bed with his trusty cane and there was the big black, hairy culprit. It was huge. The brother then placed the tin over the beast and put the lid back on the tin. I was sweating like a racehorse by this stage and probably looked as pale as pale could be.

"Stand by your beds and stop this nonsense. It will be time for lights out now," yelled Brother Dominic.

We quickly assumed our positions by our beds, and he seemed to stop behind me on his way out. Within seconds, I felt something crawling on my head. Panic set in and I ran out of the dormitory screaming like a lunatic as fast as I could to the bathroom whilst slapping my own head hard and fast. I put my head in the nearest sink and turned the tap on full in a desperate attempt to wash the bloody monster off my head.

Alec came in to the bathroom and said, "It's OK now, Tommy. The spider fell off your head by the bed and I have stamped on it now, so it's dead."

I managed to calm myself down enough to go back to the dormitory, where I found Brother Dominic with a smile from ear to ear on his face.

"Now look at Porter, everybody. He is scared of spiders! They are God's little creatures and he is scared of them," said Brother Dominic sarcastically.

"Where did you find the spider?" he asked. "We found it under a box of wine when we were clearing out the church cellar today, Sir. We were only playing a joke on our Tommy," Alec replied.

"As it was you lot that had been helping Father Simon earlier today, I will let you off this time for the commotion, but if there's any more nonsense tonight, then I will not be so lenient. If there's any more, then I will deal with you first, Porter," were his parting words whilst slapping his cane against his leg on his way out of the dormitory.

Alec and the boys came over to my bed just before lights out and apologised for putting the spider in the tin. They said that they did not realize how frightened I was of spiders and they promised never to do it again. To this day, I am an arachnophobe and later in life found out that some of my brothers were also scared of spiders. I think that was the only thing they were scared of.

Chapter Twenty-Two

Wales...Where the Hell is that?

Summer came around again and expectations were high amongst us boys with regard to the possibility of going to another summer camp. Last year's event had been so much fun and everyone really enjoyed getting out of the school for a little holiday. Nothing had been mentioned about a summer camp, so I asked brother David if we were going again. Brother David told me that the headmaster was meeting with the social services and that he would let me know if there were any developments concerning summer camp or anything else. At the time, I didn't really think too much about his comments about the meeting with the social services and just assumed it was a routine meeting.

The sunny days passed us by and life at the school was better than ever. Alec seemed to spend every spare moment playing football and he had been selected to play for the school team. Alec was a very good goalkeeper and he also was a regular in the school cross-country team. I was able to go on free walks regularly, and really enjoyed the independence. On these unaccompanied walks, I would sometimes bump into some of the former pupils of the school, who would come back to visit. Every time I met any former pupils, I tried to find out as much information about the hostel in London as possible, as I knew that it would one day be my next home.

Opinions of the hostel were not the best, but I thought it was better to find out than to go there one day unprepared. All the boys said that you had to watch your back in the hostel, as there were all sorts of people coming and going. They would be encouraged to go out to work all day (and pay rent for the accommodation) and had to share a large room with others at night. There was no dining hall, and they had to eat out. Every one of the former pupils I spoke to said that they were desperately trying to save up to rent a room somewhere else when they could. Despite the grim tales of hostel life, every time I thought about leaving my younger brother Alec, I felt sick. I knew that one day this would have to happen, and it bothered me immensely.

Before I knew it, August seemed to creep up on me. The headmaster summoned us all to the recreation hall for an announcement. Great, we all thought, summer camp here we come! Excitement echoed around the walls of the hall until the headmaster delivered his message to us all. St Joseph's School had not been selected to attend this year's summer camp as another school from Kent had been selected instead. Hearts sank and there was a notable groan of disappointment from the boys. In an attempt to compensate for this disappointing blow, the headmaster went on to say that he would arrange a sports day at the school and that he would invite teams from other schools to come and compete against those of St Joseph's. This did little to raise our spirits. The sports day took place at the end of August, and it passed with little significance. We all missed the trip out on the bus, the ferry journey and the adventure of sleeping under canvas.

A few weeks later, I had just finished clearing up after breakfast when one of the brothers told me to go to the headmaster's office, as he wanted to see me. I racked my brains to think what I had done wrong to merit such a trip of inevitable despair.

"What have you done Tommy?" Alec immediately asked.

"I'll tell you when I get back, Alec," I said as I began walking out of the dining hall accompanied by the brother. When we reached the headmaster's office, I was told to sit down on the chair outside the room and to wait quietly until I was called in.

I waited patiently outside the headmaster's office for what seemed to be ages. A brother then appeared and took a bundle of papers into the office. I remained puzzled as to what this meeting was about. The brother then emerged from the office without the papers and he told me that I would soon be seen. A few minutes later, the door to the office swung open and the headmaster, Brother Peter, said, "Come in, Thomas."

As I entered the office, I was greeted by the sight of two strangers, a man and a woman, sitting at either end of the headmaster's meeting table, with the headmaster sitting in the middle. I stood there with a tremble in my knees and a somewhat startled look on my face.

"Sit in the chair, Thomas. We need to talk to you," said the headmaster before he introduced me to the official looking strangers.

"This is Thomas John Porter," he told them.

"Thomas. You will be 15 years of age on the 23 September, which is next month. As a result, it will then be time for you to leave St Joseph's School and to make your way in the world," he told me as I sat nervously in the chair.

I wanted to answer him, but I just couldn't speak. My words would not come out of my mouth, which now felt as dry as an old piece of leather. The thought of having to leave Alec behind hit me like a hammer blow. I felt sick.

The man who by now I had guessed was from social services, went on to say without showing any emotion on his face, "It has been decided by social services that you will leave St Joseph's School at the end of this September. You will be accommodated at a hostel in Hackney, London, and we have found a job for you. You will be required to work with the local council in their parks and gardens department. You will be provided with footwear and clothes for work."

At this point, my mouth and brain reengaged and I managed to say, "Why can't I go home to Bootle and to my family?"

The woman then piped up and said, "Thomas, none of your family in Liverpool want you or your brother Alec."

I sat there crying as my mind tried to comprehend what the woman had just said to me. Surely this could not be true, I thought to myself, as Alec and I returning to our family in Bootle had been the main focus that had kept us going since the day we were taken away from our family home.

"It is for your own good, Thomas. The social services will look after you and maybe one day when you are older, you can return to Liverpool," the headmaster said in an attempt to comfort me.

"What about Alec? What will happen to him when I leave St Joseph's?" I blubbered.

"Alec will have to stay here with the Christian brothers until he is 15. Maybe then he can be with you again. Have you any more questions?" the woman said.

I sat there with my head down sobbing, and did not answer. I was distressed, as the thought of leaving my brother was simply terrible. We had always been together and had comforted each other during the tough times we had met. The man then told me that they would be back in two weeks after they had made all the necessary arrangements for me to leave. I left the room devastated.

As opposed to returning to the recreation hall, I took myself off to the church. Here I sat at a pew at the back on my own and I sobbed my heart out. I felt so lonely, unwanted and scared. I closed my eyes and desperately prayed to God for him not to let the authorities split Alec and I up. As I wept uncontrollably whilst sitting at the back of the cold church, I jumped as I felt an arm being placed around my shoulders. I looked to find Father Simon sitting next to me.

"What is the matter, Thomas?" he asked.

I explained what had been said at the meeting and how I was struggling with the thoughts that were revolving in my mind as a result. Father Simon and I sat and talked for over an hour. Father Simon made me feel a little better about it all, as he had said that I could come back and visit Alec at the weekend and that he would look out for Alec once I had left.

"Let's go back to the recreational hall, Thomas, as everyone will be wondering where you have gone," Father Simon concluded.

Father Simon, who walked with me with his arm still around my shoulder to the recreation hall, then explained to Brother John, who was on the door of the hall, that I was upset and he had found me praying in the church. Brother John sent me up to the dormitory, where Alec was waiting for me.

"Where have you been, Tommy? I thought you had run away without me," said Alec.

This started my tears off again.

I sat on Alec's bed in the dormitory and explained to him what was going to happen to us next. As predicted, Alec was heartbroken, and we both cried.

"Don't worry, Alec. I will go and live in the hostel in Hackney and when I get my first payday, I will come back and we can run away together to somewhere where they will never find us," I told him.

Our spirits lifted with this plan and I went on to say, "We can't run away to Granny Porter's, though, as she called the police last time, remember."

We both raised a smile and hugged each other. I could have hugged him forever and didn't want to let him go. The dormitory lights were put out and we both got into our beds. I remember lying there awake all night, as the thought of leaving my little brother in this place was burning into my mind's eye.

The next two weeks were hell for me as the time to leave drew closer and closer. I withdrew from what little impersonation of society that existed in the school and I did not want to mix with or talk to anyone. The slightest thing would upset me. The boys who were my friends understood how I was feeling and left me alone to come to terms with the demons in my head.

Whilst I sat, uninterested, in class one day, Brother David entered the room and he asked me to accompany him to the headmaster's office. I broke out into a cold sweat as I walked along the corridor to the office. When I arrived, I saw Alec sitting on the chair outside the room.

"What's going on, Tommy?" asked Alec.

I shrugged my shoulders, as again I was lost for words. I joined Alec and took a seat in the corridor outside the headmaster's office whilst Brother David went inside.

Father Simon opened the door to the office and told us to enter and to take a seat. Alec and I sat down on the old wooden chairs in front of what appeared to be a panel of six people; made up of the headmaster, Brother David, Father Simon, the two social services people whom I had met at the last meeting and a man that I had never seen before.

The headmaster, brother Peter opened with, "I have called you both into my office today as there has been a slight change to the arrangements regarding Thomas leaving St Joseph's School. I will leave it to the Ms Deadron to explain."

I looked at Alec, and we both waited eagerly to learn the news.

"I have some good news for you both," the woman from social services said as she looked at me.

'"You were informed last time we met that you would be going to live in the hostel in Hackney in London, however, thanks to the efforts of Father Simon and the Catholic Church, we have managed to contact one of your sisters, Edith Edwards. Mrs Edwards lives in Wales and she is willing to accept you both into her home with her husband and child."

This was the best news we could have wished for. "Wales....where's that?" I asked as I look at Alec, who now had a beaming smile on his face. The woman smiled at us both and went to say, "Your sister is married and is now living in Wales. You are not able to leave until November, as she is expecting another child. You will then be transferred into the care of North Wales social services, who will seek work for you. Alec will be able to spend Christmas with you in Wales, however, he will then have to return to St Joseph's where he will remain until he is 15 years of age."

The man from social services then asked, "Is this what you would like to happen?"

Before he had finished his sentence, both Alec and I shouted in stereo, "Yes! Yes, please!"

"I am very pleased for you both." Father Simon told us with a warm smile on his face as Alec and I left the office very happy boys. We could not wait to tell our friends the good news when we got back to the dormitory. Alec and I could hardly believe that we were going to home to our big sister Edie, albeit in a place called Wales, wherever that may be. Alec and I both slept contently that night with the warm feeling of being reunited with our sister.

As the next few weeks came and went, all I could think of was going to live in this place called Wales. It was a Monday when we were both called to the headmaster's office again. We knew that this was it. We were going to find out when we would leave St Joseph's and see our sister again.

When we arrived at the headmaster's office, we were greeted by Brother Peter and three men in suits whom we had not seen before. Alec and I were then informed that we would be leaving St Josephs at 7 am on Friday and that we were to be given train tickets. Mine was to be a single and Alec's a return, as he had to come back to the school after Christmas. I could see Alec was starting to get upset, so in an attempt to take his mind off it, I asked, "Exactly how will we get to Wales?"

"You will catch the train at Orpington station to Paddington. From there, you'll get on a train to Crewe, change trains to Chester and then on to a place called Barmouth, where your sister lives," one of the social services men replied.

"We will give you the train times and numbers and a letter for you to give to the station masters if you get stuck. Your sister Edith will meet you at the station in Barmouth," he added.

Alec and I did not ask any questions, as we were over the moon with the thought of finally leaving the school and seeing a member of our family again.

"I will see you before you leave, and I will then give you the tickets and instructions," the headmaster said before we were told to leave the office.

The rest of that week we were excused from attending lessons as we busily returned all school property, such as our clothes and sports kit, to the relevant parts of the school. The day before we were set to leave the school, Alec and I were issued with new clothes to travel in and a small, tatty suitcase, in which we packed our pyjamas, underpants, vests and socks. We were ready to leave and could not wait!

Later that day, we were again called to the headmaster's office. Here, the headmaster handed me an envelope containing the train tickets and a list of stations and train times that related to our forthcoming journey.

"I hope you will be happy in your new home, Thomas, and if you ever return to Kent, I hope you will call in to see us at St Joseph's School. I will not see you in the morning, so I will say my goodbye now. Good luck, Thomas. Brother Dominic will escort you both to the gates at 7 in the morning," the headmaster said.

"Thank you, Sir. I will definitely come back to visit," I replied, as I thought to myself that I would never set foot in this place again.

To his credit the headmaster, Brother Peter, had been a strict but fair individual. It was a shame this could not be said about all the Christian brothers.

After leaving the headmaster's office, Alec and I went for our final supper at the dining hall. Word had got around that the Porter boys were leaving in the morning, and I remember being surprised by how many of the boys came over to wish us both well and to say goodbye to us. All the boys who sat at our table made a promise that someday we would all meet up again, although I knew in my heart that this would never happen.

Friday morning arrived quickly, and I was wide awake before dawn, but I had to stay in bed until 6 am. Alec and I went to the bathroom, washed, and then got dressed in our new clothes. We felt special in our new shirts, jumpers, long trousers and grey coats. We looked so different to the attire of the other boys that day. Once dressed in our new clobber, we rolled up our mattresses and placed them neatly at the end of our beds before putting our bed sheets into the laundry basket.

On our way to the dining hall, we bumped into Brother David in the corridor, who said, "I wish you both all the luck in this world and I hope you will be happy."

Brother David had been kind to both of us, and we really enjoyed his sports lessons, so I guess we were a little sad to say goodbye to him.

My brother and I then began our walk to the dining hall for what was my final breakfast in the school. An expressionless Brother Dominic was waiting for us at the top of the stairs, as he was to escort us to breakfast and then to the gates of the school. I could not eat much of my breakfast, as my stomach was doing somersaults with the excitement of going to live with my sister Edie. I said goodbye to the boys who had sat on my table in the dining hall and could not wait to leave.

After breakfast, we made our way to collect our suitcase. On the way, a couple of the boys who were cleaning the staircase stopped work briefly to shout, "Goodbye, Tommy and Alec."

Before we could exchange pleasantries with the boys, brother Dominic shouted in his loud voice, "Quiet, you lot. Just get on with your work. No talking on the stairs."

Ironically, these were the very same words, spoken by the very same brother that had greeted us when we first arrived at St Joseph's School.

Brother John was waiting for us by the main door and he gave me an envelope containing two pounds and 10 shillings. This was the amount we had amassed in our saving books. Brother John then wished us both well and said goodbye, before we were escorted along the long driveway to the main gates of the school by Brother Dominic. He did not speak to either of us whilst he walked with us and when we arrived at the school gates and as he opened them, he said, "Porter, I am glad to see the back of you."

He then looked at Alec and said, "I will see you when you return."

Not if I have anything to do with it, I thought to myself. I did not answer him and Alec and I walked as fast as we could away from the school.

I never looked back at the school and my mind was now set on getting on the right trains and getting to Wales to see our sister Edie. I knew my way to the railway station at Orpington as I had passed it a few times during my free walks. I was carrying the suitcase and Alec walked beside me whilst holding on to my sleeve, as he did when he was anxious. We walked briskly until we reached the railway station in the town.

When we got to the station, I went up to an official-looking chap in uniform and showed him our tickets and letter and asked him if he could help us find the right train.

"Is anyone travelling with you, boys?" He asked. "No, Sir." I replied. The man shook his head in disbelief, and said, "The next train arriving at this platform is the one you want. Sit on the bench, boys, and I will tell you when to board the train. You then stay on this train until you get to Paddington."

The train arrived, the man waved us on and we got on the train. As it pulled out of the station, I pulled the window down and waved to the guard. He waved back, and our journey to Barmouth had started. Alec and I sat in the corridor of the train by a window; Alec on one side of the suitcase and me on the other, guarding it as if it contained the Crown jewels. All the possessions we had in the world were being worn or in the tatty old brown suitcase.

The train arrived at what appeared to be a huge railway station. Paddington was bigger than I had imagined. We remained on the train until all the other passengers had got off and I asked the ticket inspector where we needed to go next. He looked at our letter and he said, "OK, boys. Come with me. I'll sort it for you."

The man took us to a smoke-filled room in the station, where the guards and other officials were sitting drinking tea and smoking cigarettes. He then asked one of the men sitting in the room to make sure that we got to Crewe.

"Look out for them, please, as these boys are travelling on their own," the man said to his colleague, who was puffing on his cigarette like there was no tomorrow.

We declined their kind invitation to wait for the train with them in the smoke-filled staff room and we sat quietly on the bench outside waiting for our train.

The train to Crewe arrived in a cloud of steam, and both Alec and I boarded without a problem. One of the men from the staff room spoke to the guard on the train to ask him to make sure we got to Crewe and then got off for the train to Chester. That was very kind, I thought to myself. The train was rammed full of people, so we took turns to sit on the suitcase in the corridor. I did not care if we had to sit on the roof of the train, as all that I could think of was going to live with my sister in Barmouth. The other passengers may have thought us a little odd, as we even took our suitcase to the toilet when we needed to go, but we did not care.

I have no idea how long the journey that day took, but it seemed like a very long time. Alec and I passed the time by looking at the scenery out of the window. We were excited, as we had never been on a steam train as paying passengers before. The only other time we had been on a steam train was when we had run away from Radcliff and hidden under the seats, until Alec burnt his leg on the heater pipe and we got caught at Crewe station. I was hoping that this visit to Crewe was going to be less eventful. Like the fascinating scenery, the hours passed us by and the train sounded its whistle as it entered Crewe station. Then the guard came to find us and said, "This is it, boys. You get off here and change trains for Chester. Come with me and I will have a word with one of the platform staff and make sure you get your next connection."

The guard then took us to the office on Crewe station, where he went in to speak with someone for Alec and I. "It's all sorted. The guard on your next train will be told that you need to get to Chester and he will look after you," he said when he came out.

Again, we declined his kind offer to go into the office to wait for the train and we opted to wait on the bench. I did not want to show my face in that office, as it had been the very same one in which they had detained us until the police turned up when we got caught running away previously. I was worried in case someone recognised us, and then they would not help us get to Barmouth.

Alec and I sat on a bench at the far end of Crewe station until our train arrived. Again, the guard checked our tickets and read our letter. We then boarded the train for the next leg of our journey. It did not take long for our train to reach Chester. Once we arrived, the guard again went to check on the time of our next connection, which was the final leg of our journey and would take us to Barmouth itself, where our sister would be waiting for us.

"The train to Barmouth is on time boys. It's due here in 20 minutes, so get on it when it arrives," said the guard as he walked away and left us sitting there on the station.

A train soon appeared and came to a stop at our platform. I asked a woman who was also waiting on the platform if it was the train to Barmouth as Alec tugged my sleeve again. Darkness had now fallen and we boarded the train for our final leg of the journey. Alec and I resumed our seating position, taking it in turns to sit on the suitcase in the corridor of the train. It was dark, and we could no longer see the passing scenery, but we didn't care, as the excitement of being reunited with a family member took priority over everything.

The steam train trundled on down the Welsh tracks and several strangely-named stations that were impossible to pronounce came and went as Alec and I sat on our tatty brown suitcase. At one station, several workers got on, and one of the men approached us and asked, "Are you the Porter boys that are travelling to Barmouth, by any chance?"

"Yes, Sir, we are," I replied.

"Well, come and sit in the carriage with us if you like," he added.

I politely declined and was totally confused. How did he know who we were and where we were going? This was weird.

With our eyes glued to the darkness outside of the window, our train came to another stop. This time, we saw the word Barmouth on the sign.

"Alec, we're here!" I said enthusiastically as I quickly grabbed the suitcase and quickly shuffled along the corridor to the door in preparation to get off the train.

"No, boys, this is not your stop. Your stop is Barmouth, and this is Barmouth Junction," the worker shouted out to us.

"It's the next stop," he added.

I felt my heart skip a beat, as I knew we were not far away now.

As the train pulled away from Barmouth Junction station, we soon realised that the train was making its way over a large bridge, as we could see water below us out of the window. Alec and I were even more excited now, as we had never travelled over water before by train. The only other time we had been across water had been as stowaways on the ferry across the River Mersey years before.

We crossed what seemed to be a huge patch of water and the train snaked around some rocks until it came to a halt at Barmouth station. The kind worker shouted as he and his workmates left the train, "OK, boys, this is your stop. This is Barmouth."

I grabbed our suitcase and we got off the train on to the deserted and dark station platform. The workers seemed to have disappeared into the night, and we were all alone, with no sign of my sister.

"Are we in the right place, Tommy?" Alec said nervously as he tugged my sleeve yet again.

Before I had chance to answer him, we saw the lone figure of a man emerging from the darkness and walking towards us. Alec tugged my sleeve harder, and I gripped our suitcase firmly. Was this man going to steal our suitcase? The man got closer to us and I still could not see his face. The man then went to take the suitcase from my hands and said, "Hello, boys."

I pulled the suitcase away as hard as I could and the man responded in a soft Scouse voice, "It's alright, Tommy. It's me...Paddy. Your brother."

I was overcome with the shock of seeing my brother Paddy again. I was expecting to see my sister Edie at the station, and I had not seen Paddy for over four years. I relaxed my grip on the suitcase and Paddy took hold of it and put his arm around my shoulder as we began to walk to the exit of the station. I wept as we walked. I was so happy to be reunited with our Paddy.

"Where's Edie?" I asked.

"It's alright, Tommy, don't worry. Edie is waiting for you at her house. It's only down the road," Paddy replied.

We felt safe now we had our Paddy with us. It had been a long time since we had spent time with our brother Paddy. Oh, how we had missed him.

We then left the darkness of Barmouth station and continued to walk along the streets of the small seaside town of Barmouth for the first time.

"How was your journey here? Have you had something to eat?" asked Paddy.

"We've not eaten anything since six o clock this morning. We just wanted to get here, and food was the last thing on my mind," Alec said.

Our route to Edie's house took us off the main street of the town and we began to climb what seemed to be hundreds of old stone steps in the pitch black of the night. We stayed close to our Paddy as we climbed the steps.

"Edie lives up here on the rock. We'll be there in a few minutes," Paddy reassured us.

We eventually reached a terrace of what appeared to be small stone cottages, and Paddy knocked on the door. The door opened and we were greeted by a tearful woman whom I recognised immediately as my eldest sister, Edie.

"They're here!" screamed Edie as she threw her arms around Alec and I.

The tears flowed as we stood on the front doorstep, so much that some of the neighbours came out to see what all the fuss was about. We all went inside Edie's house and we sat crying and talking for hours and hours. I was at last reunited with some of my family, and words simply cannot express how I felt.

Paddy never came in and told us he would see us tomorrow – he disappeared into the darkness as quickly as he had appeared.

Chapter Twenty-Three

Barmouth

After our tearful reunion and what seemed like hours of talking with our sister Edie, she took us to another house called Green Bank. This was the home of her mother-in-law, Mrs Edwards and this was where Alec and I were to stay. There simply was not enough room for us at Edie's small stone cottage.

"Where is Paddy going to sleep?" I asked Edie as we walked to Green Bank.

"Paddy will be alright. Don't worry about him," Edie replied.

When we reached Green Bank, Alec and I were impressed, as we had our own bedroom. We had what seemed to be a huge bed in the room with two mattresses. Alec and I got washed and got into bed. The bed was comfortable, but seemed to be very high off the floor. It was different to the beds we had been used to sleeping in. We really didn't care, though, as Alec and I were finally reunited with some of our family. We chatted excitedly into the early hours. We were so happy to be with Paddy, Edie and Aggie again. Edie had told us that were going to see Aggie the next day.

The morning came and we both woke up happier than we had been for many years. It was still dark outside, and there was silence in the house. Mrs Edwards and her son, Lewis, lived in Green Bank, so we were careful not to wake them up. The rule of not talking whilst in the dormitory was what we had been used to, so I whispered to Alec, "Let's get dressed and go downstairs."

Once dressed, Alec and I crept down the narrow staircase as quietly as we could. I poked my head around the door of the kitchen that stood ajar, but there was nobody to be seen. Alec followed me on tiptoes towards the front door. I tried the handle and to my surprise the door opened. I simply could not resist this opportunity to go outside and, although daylight was just breaking, to explore our new home of Barmouth.

Green Bank was situated in an elevated position, and it overlooked the town. The front garden was small, with a little stone wall that appeared to have quite a drop on the other side of it. We could see the lights of what was obviously the town of Barmouth. There was a harbour with lots of small boats bobbing on the water in view and a beach that seemed to go on forever.

"Wow. Look at this, Alec. This place looks amazing," I said quietly to my brother. "Let's go and have a look."

It had been dark when we arrived at Green Bank, so we didn't know how to get down to the town and harbour, but we just had to try. The old rickety wooden gate creaked as I opened it. Alec remained close to my side as we walked down a narrow path on what seemed to be a mountain. The drop on the other side of the path seemed to get bigger, so we were pleased when the sun continued to rise slowly in the sky and thus gave us more light. We soon came across a large church that seemed to be built almost into the mountain. It featured a large clock that told us it was 6.30 am.

"Do you think we'd better get back to the house, Tommy? Someone may be looking for us by now," Alec said nervously.

"Let's just go a bit further, Alec. I wonder if that is a Catholic church," I replied.

"Well, if it is a Catholic church, there may be brothers there, and they will catch us." Alec was quick to point out.

"Good point. Let's walk behind the church so nobody will see us," I answered.

The path behind the church seemed to snake further back up the mountain. I began to worry that we were going to end up lost in the hills, so I decided to take us on a route that seemed to head down towards the lights of the town. Our path eventually led us to a row of small houses that stood on a narrow street. Alec was now tugging my sleeve once again, so I knew he was a little anxious.

"Tommy, we have been away from the house for some time now and we haven't seen anyone," Alec piped up.

As he did, a man appeared from nowhere and said,

"Are you Tommy and Alec Porter?"

"Yes, Sir." I nervously replied.

"Your sister Edie has been looking for you. Come with me and I will take you to her," the man said in a deep voice.

This man guided us down lots of stone steps until we came to what seemed to be a street in the town. To our relief, Paddy and Edie were standing there waiting for us. Edie was upset, and she asked, "Where the hell have you been? We've been looking everywhere for you."

"Sorry, Edie. It's my fault, not Alec's. We couldn't sleep, so we thought we would have a look around and we got lost," I replied sheepishly.

Edie gave us both a big hug and said,

"Let's go home."

As we walked through the streets of Barmouth for the very first time, lots of people stopped and were asking Edie if we were the brothers that had come to stay with her. Edie told all of them what had happened on our first morning and everyone laughed, with most saying, "How can you get lost in Barmouth?"

When we got back to Edie's cottage, she said, "Tommy, you can go wherever you like, but please just let us know first. We were all worried about you both."

The box room in Edie's small stone cottage, 3 Goronwy Terrace, on the rock was to be converted into a bedroom for Alec and I, however, Mrs Edwards' house (Green Bank) was where we were to stay until then. Mrs Edwards was very kind to us. It was a little strange living in somebody's house, but at least we didn't have that nasty Brother Dominic waking us up every morning with his unique cheerful disposition.

From our new home on the rock, we could taste the sea air and we could see what looked like a busy little harbour full of fishing boats. The sea air took me back to our time in Bootle and I could not wait to get a chance to go and explore the harbour area of the town. On our first morning at Goronwy Terrace, after we had breakfast, I asked my sister Edie,

"Can we go to look at the harbour please?"

"Tommy, you can't go down to the harbour without an adult. Wait until Paddy arrives, he will take you there, I am sure," she replied.

"Where does our Paddy live?" I asked.

"Paddy lives in town. He will come for you tomorrow and he'll take you to the harbour," replied Edie.

The next day, Paddy came and had breakfast with us. I was pleased to see him and was instantly excited about getting a chance to see the boats on the harbour.

"We are going to take you both to see Aggie today," Edie said.

The boats were quickly forgotten as Alec and I looked at each other with grins that stretched from ear to ear. I wondered if I would recognise my sister Aggie, as it had been years since I had seen her.

"Do any other of our brothers and sisters live in Barmouth, Edie?" I asked as I tried to contain my excitement of seeing Aggie once again.

"No Tommy. They are still in Liverpool," Edie responded.

Breakfast was over and myself, Alec, Edie and Paddy walked down the narrow stone steps from the rock into the town. Barmouth was busy and all of the locals seemed very friendly. As we walked to meet Aggie, lots of people stopped to talk to Edie to ask if Alec and I were settling in okay. I was surprised and a little taken aback that so many people knew of Alec and I.

Having walked through what we were told was the main high street of the town, we arrived at a large hotel situated on a small hill, The Royal Hotel. Edie went and spoke to an official-looking man at the reception, who came up and introduced himself as the hotel manager.

"You must be the boys that I have heard so much about. Agnes will be pleased to see you. Follow me," he said as he showed us up a posh-looking staircase.

Once on the first floor, we arrived at one of the hotel rooms. The manager knocked on the door and said, "Agnes, there is someone here to see you."

The door swung open and there she stood: our sister Aggie.

"Oh my God," Aggie shouted loudly, "they're here!"

She threw her arms around Alec and I and we sat crying on what was her bed at the hotel. I will never forget seeing our Aggie for the first time in years. She looked so posh in her hotel uniform. It was quite a contrast to her days as a tomboy fighting alongside Paddy and Siddy McKevitt on the streets of Bootle. The last recollection I had of her before that day was one of her happily swinging on the lamppost on Marsh Lane with her skirt tucked in her drawers!

"I'm so sorry that I didn't meet you from the train. We were very busy in the hotel, and I couldn't get the time off," Aggie said.

"It's okay Aggie," I reassured her. "We understand and are so happy to be back together again."

We spent most of the afternoon sitting with Aggie, talking about where we had been and what had been happening in each of our lives during the years we had been apart. Later that afternoon, Edie told us that we had a meeting with a social worker called Mrs Jones, who was responsible for Alec and I and had to oversee Alec's return to St Joseph's after the Christmas holiday of 1955. Every time we thought of Alec going back to St Joseph's, our hearts sank a little.

"Come on then, boys. We need to go to see Mrs Jones. She lives on Porkington Terrace, so let's get going," Edie said later that afternoon.

Alec and I nervously accompanied Edie back through the main street of Barmouth and up past the harbour area to Porkington Terrace, which was a terraced row of large, impressive, houses that overlooked the sea and the wooden bridge that we had crossed in the train on our journey to Barmouth. Mrs Jones seemed like a pleasant but stern character who was straight talking. We entered her house and sat in the front room.

Mrs Jones opened the meeting with, "During the time that you are under my charge, you must obey all of the conditions set out by the social services."

Mrs Jones went on to reel off a list of conditions, most of which Alec and I did not really understand. I knew that we had to behave and not to get into any trouble while we were living in Barmouth. I was determined that we would not slip up, as the thought of getting sent back to one of those establishments was terrible.

"Mrs Jones, is it possible for Alec to stay with Tommy in Barmouth and not to be taken back to St Joseph's after Christmas?" Edie enquired hopefully as the butterflies in my stomach awoke once more.

"Edie, it is not a decision I can make, unfortunately. It will be up to the authorities as to where Alec goes, but I will make enquiries and I will let you know of course." She replied as Alec and I broke down and cried. "Please don't cr,y boys. I will do my best for you,"

Mrs Jones said as the meeting ended.

Mrs Jones said her goodbyes and off we walked with heavy hearts once more. Just as I thought things were getting better for Alec and I, it seemed Alec would probably be taken away and back to St Joseph's after Christmas. The thought of Alec not being with me bothered me immensely. I was determined to show the authorities that we were good children who simply wanted to be with their family.

As time passed, we tried to put the threat of Alec having to go back to St Joseph's on his own after Christmas to the back of our minds, as we had fun playing and getting to know the other local children. Despite getting lost on our first day in Barmouth and experiencing a strange feeling of freedom, Alec and I settled quickly into our new lives. The inhabitants of the town of Barmouth were a friendly bunch, and they all made us feel very welcome.

Everybody stopped to say hello and to ask us about ourselves, and the children who lived on the rock would invite us in to their houses to play. Barmouth seemed to have a strong community spirit, and lots of ladies with their children popped in to see our sister Edie, which was great, as Alec and I soon got to know the names of some of the local children.

As we were newcomers to the seaside town, the locals spoke to us in English, however, when most of them conversed with each other, they did so in a strange language that we had never heard before: Welsh. It sounded quite amusing when they rattled off deep into conversation, although Alec and I contained our amused grins, as we did not want to offend.

At last, life was good once again. Summer came and went and the Christmas of 1955 was looming. I wondered what this Christmas had in store for Alec and I. The other children that had befriended us all talked about receiving presents, but all I really wanted for Christmas was to still have my younger brother Alec with me.

Christmas Eve arrived and Edie asked me to look after her baby, Christine, whilst her and her husband went to the Crown Hotel for a drink with all of the other mothers and fathers. This was apparently customary at that time. Edie assured me that they would be back after the pubs closed at 9 pm. I was terrified, as I had never looked after a baby before. I reluctantly agreed to look after Christine, as I knew that the pub was at the bottom of the steps and Alec could get there quickly to notify Edie if there was a problem.

Edie gave her instructions and left Alec and I with the baby and went off for a festive drink or two at the pub. Initially it seemed easy, this babysitting lark, until baby Christine woke up and started crying. Both Alec and I tried our best to console the baby and passed back and forth, holding her in our arms and rocking her gently to try and stop the crying. Our efforts were to no avail, and we were so glad when Edie returned later that evening and settled her baby.

Alec and I went to bed really excited on this Christmas Eve. We had both dreamed of being reunited with our family again, and sharing a Christmas with them once more. Now it was really happening. Christmas morning soon came, and Alec and I were not disappointed. There seemed to be lots of presents for us from Edie, Paddy and Aggie. Most of the gifts were clothes for us both, and we were very pleased as we had only the clothes we had come to town in.

Later that day, Paddy came around to the house to wish us a merry Christmas, and he stayed for Christmas dinner. Our sister Aggie could not make it, as she had to work in the hotel serving Christmas dinner to the customers. We knew that she would be straight around to see us once her shift at the hotel had finished. After enjoying a hearty Christmas dinner, Alec and I went out to play with the other children.

The evening was spent listening to our sister Edie talking about the rest of the family back in Liverpool and our younger siblings Joan, Ritchie and Kathleen.

Alec and I were desperate to know what had happened to everyone.

"Where are Ritchie, Joan and Kathleen?" I asked.

"I really don't know, Tommy. Nobody has seen them since they had been taken away," Edie replied.

Edie did not know the whereabouts of Joan, Ritchie and Kathleen, and my mind raced back to the places that Alec and I had been taken to. I silently prayed that they were in a nicer place than the schools we had been in. By this time, we were all crying. As the tears started to flow, Paddy got up and said his goodbyes, before he left the cottage and walked off into the darkness once again.

"Where does Paddy live?" I asked Edie.

"Paddy does not live far away. He lives with a Mr and Mrs Tommy Owen in Water Street," she replied.

Having enjoyed a lovely Christmas day, Alec and I thanked Edie for the presents and for our dinner before we left to return to Mrs Edwards' house. I lay in the big bed in Green Bank and whilst Alec dropped off to sleep with a content look upon his face, I could not help myself from thinking about the prospect of Alec having to return to St Josephs. I remembered he had a return ticket and thus, did not sleep much that night.

A week or so later, as Alec and I were playing on the stone steps on the rock with our friends, Edie appeared and said, "Come inside, boys, and change your clothes. We are off to see Mrs Jones the social worker."

My heart instantly sank. Alec and I went into the cottage and as we were getting changed, Alec said with a tear in his eye, "Are you coming back to St Joseph's with me, Tommy?"

"You are not going back there on your own, Alec. Even if we have to run away again. Don't worry," I replied.

Once changed, we accompanied my sister Edie and her husband, Ronnie Edwards, to an office in Barmouth town centre. Alec tugged on my sleeve as we walked down the steps to the office. We were both as white as a sheet and very nervous. Upon arrival at this office, Alec and I were told to take a seat outside whilst the adults went into the room. We sat there for seemed like an eternity, with our hearts in our mouths and stomachs in knots. Suddenly, a man that we had never seen before emerged from the office and showed Alec and I into the room.

Alec and I sat down at the end of a long, polished official-looking wooden table as we waited to hear what fate had in store next for us. I racked my memory, but I was certain that we had behaved ourselves since leaving St Joseph's. I was worried sick, but I glanced over at my sister Edie and she was smiling, so that made me feel a little better about the situation.

Mrs Jones, the social worker, stood up at the front of the table and said, "Boys, we have some good news for you both." Alec and I grinned nervously at each other.

"When you left St Joseph's School, you were told that Alec would have to return to the school after the

Christmas holiday," Mrs Jones said, as Alec and I began to tremble with anxiety.

"I am pleased to inform you that there has been a change in circumstances and it has been decided by the social services that you both will remain together in Barmouth and you will live with Mr and Mrs Edwards," she went on to say.

I reached over and hugged Alec and we both cried tears of joy and relief.

"Your sister Edie told social services that it was not fair to split you both up now, as you had been together since the death of your parents in Liverpool. Edie had said that if Alec were to go back to St Joseph's, then Tommy would have to also," Mrs Jones continued. "I have been appointed as your social worker, and you will both remain in the care of social services until you have both reached the age of 16. You must attend the local school and you must behave. We will be having regular meetings to monitor your progress."

Alec and I were now sobbing our little hearts out and I am sure that some of the officials in the room were fighting back the tears. The adults continued to talk to Edie, but I could not take on board any more information, as I was ecstatic that we were staying together and we would be with our family at long last.

Mrs Jones asked if we had any questions, so I plucked up the courage and asked, "Do I have to go to school, as I am now 15?"

"You are under the care of social services and must attend school until we find suitable work for you, Thomas," Mrs Jones replied.

I was more than happy with this arrangement, as long as my brother and I remained together in this wonderful new home called Barmouth.

I knew then that the bond would never be broken.

<u>Micky, Johnny and Stevie all married, had children and remained in Bootle for the rest of their days. My eldest sister, Edie married and later moved to Crewe. Mary married and raised a family in Bootle. Aggie married and remained in Barmouth for the rest of her life. Alec stayed in Barmouth for many years before moving to Crewe, he married and had children. Joan came from the orphanage to Barmouth to stay with Edie, however, she could not settle and moved back to Bootle. She married and went on to live her life in Londonderry in Northern Ireland. Richie had been adopted and raised by a kind family in another part of Liverpool but he returned to Bootle to live when he turned 16 and he found out that he had family there. Kathleen had also been adopted at a young age by a loving family from Wigan. It was 34 years later that we finally were reunited with Kathleen. Paddy went back to Bootle, but did not settle down until he returned to Barmouth and married a local girl and raised a family.</u>

www.ingramcontent.com/pod-product-compliance
Lightning Source LLC
LaVergne TN
LVHW041610070426
835507LV00008B/182